Praise for Peter Marber

"On the money . . . . If you want to understand globalization's future, as well as some of the reasons we got into our current financial mess, reading Marber's *Seeing the Elephant* is a great place to start."
—Craig Karmin, *Wall Street Journal*

"*Money Changes Everything* is an outstanding primer on the awesome social effects of globalization."
—David Brooks, *New York Times*

"*From Third World to World Class*...Top 10 Business Books of the Year"
—*Knight Ridder Newspapers*

"It's not just the start of a new century. It's the beginning of a seminal change in society, culture, and politics, and Peter Marber gives us the blueprint. *Money Changes Everything* should be considered essential reading."
—Michele Mitchell, CNN

"Peter Marber is an original thinker who has managed to write a genuinely original book about globalization—a subject that has been exhausted by far too many more conventional analyses. His 'macro quantum' perspective on the world spotlights the critical, unavoidable fact of infinite connections among states and people. Those connections, and the uncertainty and unpredictability they bring, also open up a world of infinite possibility."
—Anne-Marie Slaughter, President, *New America Foundation*

"*From Third World to World Class* is a fresh, in-depth, and optimistic study...Peter Marber demonstrates that the power of free markets is overtaking the intellectual pessimism of the 1980s and that over time great new economic powers will be formed."
—Walter Wriston, Former Chairman and CEO, *Citicorp*

"Reference Reading for the 24/7 Marketplace"
—*Wired*

BRAVE NEW MATH:

Information, Globalization, and New Economic Thinking in the 21st Century

Peter Marber

Foreword by
Michele Wucker

WORLD
POLICY
INSTITUTE

In cooperation with World Policy Institute,
108 West 39th Street, New York, NY 10018

Cover design by Janaina Oliveira
Cover image courtesy of Olivetti SpA

ISBN 978-1-304-78869-6 (Paperback)
ISBN 978-1-304-78871-9 (Hardback)

Second Printing

O wonder!
How many goodly creatures are there here!
How beauteous mankind is!
O brave new world,
That has such people in't.
—William Shakespeare, *The Tempest*

Contents

Acknowledgements

This book grew from a 2012 article in the *World Policy Journal*, the quarterly publication of the World Policy Institute (WPI), a think tank that recently celebrated its 50th anniversary. It's been my pleasure to work with this important community for last decade, and its work has never been more needed.

A non-partisan center for global policy analysis and thought leadership, WPI focuses on the crucial but neglected challenges and opportunities of an increasingly connected world. World Policy stresses a global perspective; innovative, transformative thinking; and diversity of ideas. I'm proud that this book is supporting a new World Policy effort, with proceeds donated to help launch future books for up-and-coming voices.

There are so many people at WPI to thank, starting with Michele Wucker for helping launch this project and write the book's foreword. Other new and old World Policy community members - Steve Schlesinger, Karl Meyer, David Andelman, Christopher Shay, Mira Kamdar, Sherle Schwenninger, John Watts, Yaffa Fredrick, among others – have been huge supporters of my ideas over the years. Indeed, with them, this book may have never been written.

While I'm not a trained economist, I have been fortunate to surround myself with many talented economists on Wall Street and at universities – too many to mention here; many are referenced in the book. However, I have three huge intellectual debts owed to three Nobel Laureates who've made time for me including Joe Stiglitz, Michael Spence, and especially the late Bob Fogel. Over the years these men and their writings have, together, helped shape much of my thinking on information, human capital and economies. Their lives' work has been hugely inspiring, always pushing the boundaries of the field – and we certainly need more of that going forward.

Many ideas in Brave New Math came from discussions so many thought leaders and writers, all around the world – also too many to mention. But the following really deserve special acknowledgement including Dan Araya, Katinka Barysch, Dick Betts, Sarah Burd-

Sharps, Tony Carnevale, John Coatsworth, Steve Coll, Tyler Cowen, Lew Daly, Charles Emmerson, Peter Feaver, Richard Florida, Esther Fuchs, Ed Glaeser, Peter Gronn, Ron Inglehart, Merit Janow, Zach Karabell, Parag Khanna, Steve Landefeld, Kristen Lewis, Rob Lieberman, Michael Lind, Branko Milanovic, Michael Mandel, Moises Naim, Ben Pauker, Danny Quah, Andy Reamer, Diane Reay, Dani Rodrik, Paul Romer, Sasskia Sassen, Gary Sick, Anne-Marie Slaughter, and Paola Maria Valenti. All have contributed intellectual bits to this discussion, and many conversations with these individuals are strewn throughout the book.

I've been fortunate to work with *The Atlantic* magazine and its new online effort *Quartz*. Kevin Dulaney, Cynthia Jeffers Klein, Mitra Kalita and Steve Clemons have been extremely supportive. Several of my policy ideas have been published with their help and encouragement.

It takes a village to produce a book like this, and there have been many who have made valuable contributions along the way. Several student interns - Kate Antrobus, Kevin Creighton, Alex Fankuchen, Brian Feldman, Alexandra Ivanov, Arthur Pang, Vanessa Singh, Alexa Juvelis-Smith, and Vicky Zhao, all labored with me over the book's underlying research, graphs and tables. Matt Kite, Kim McGinness, Jonathan Lyons, and my wife Andrea (as always!) have been extremely helpful, like fine grain sandpaper, smoothing and refining so much of my writing and thinking.

A small final disclaimer: unlike my previous writings, this short book has relatively few footnotes and endnotes. While I've embedded as many references as possible in the text and figures, I apologize that some may be missing. The book is meant to be conversational - a dialogue. Indeed, changing the current dialogue of economics is the book's simple goal.

Foreword

Five years on from the financial collapse of 2008, many people still insist that nobody saw it coming. Leaving aside the many predictions from reputable sources who warned of a financial tsunami, a subprime bubble, a housing collapse – why did so many people fail to see the trouble looming? As we ask how to avoid the next crisis, many people argue that we need better warning signals. We also need a better sense of where to look for warnings. In this respect, the financial crisis may be viewed as one of the great information failures in recent history.

Interestingly, the people who foresaw the crisis certainly weren't looking at GDP – the number that has long been the main measure of a country's economic health – or headline employment data. They were looking at credit default swap rates, consumer debt levels, skyrocketing housing prices. The sheer dizzying heights to which some assets had reached should have been a clue: what goes up must come down.

The numbers were there if you knew where to look. Even for those who saw them, however, the red flags clashed with the headline numbers of GDP and employment, which looked strong – and made it easy for investors and policy makers who may have seen other signs of trouble to pretend that it wasn't so. Yet without rising personal and government debt, the American economy would not have appeared to be so rosy. Without the impact of cheaper inputs due to newly-formed global supply chains including emerging markets, rising U.S. productivity numbers may *not* have looked so stellar. In fact, few took notice of the rise of emerging markets in the global economy in the new millennium; most had written them off as basket cases in the crisis-ridden 1990s – a shame, since globalization only intensified since then.

Even if you were to drill down in detail on the numbers behind the headline numbers, you wouldn't find a complete picture of the present and future of the economy of the United States or of the world. To really see what's happening, you need indicators measuring progress on health, education and infrastructure; the composition of the economy and the allocation of spending among productive and destructive activities; and a better way to understand the interactions among economic activities that cross borders. That's just the start.

We need sound social and economic objectives and data to create evidence-based policies that can help us meet our targets. If we're going to set goals, we need better measurements for what we're trying to achieve. If we can't see where we are, it's hard to figure out which direction we need to go. Flawed information tends to lead to bad decisions and outcomes. But how do we figure out what the right data are? That's where Brave New Math comes in.

I met Peter Marber in the early 1990s, when I was writing for *Dow Jones Emerging Markets Report*. At that time, it was hard to get the simplest data from many of the countries on my beat. If we'd drawn a graph mapping quality and frequency of data to economic progress, I'd be we would have found a strong correlation. Since then, countries have come a long way in what they report, how soon and how often. Technology has helped, but so has political will in countries that understand that the better the information is that they provide, the more investment they will attract. Woe to the country that doesn't understand that good measurement leads to investment and growth.

Argentina, which over the past decade has sent a strong and clear message that it doesn't care what investors think, started fudging its numbers so badly that *The Economist* refused to print them. China, whose top leaders have recognized crucial flaws in its data, stopped reporting some numbers and adjusted the formulas of others, making the data even more confusing.

Investors focus on China's GDP growth, yet few of them will tell you they have any confidence in the accuracy of the numbers. Who can blame them when authorities at the highest levels of China's government agree that the data are a mess? By some measures, the main GDP number may be off by as much as one-sixth. Many analysts have searched far and wide for other ways to measure trends in China– looking at, say, electricity consumption as a proxy for economic activity- and thus get a better picture of the present and the future. One worthy effort to make sense of China's economy, the China Beige Book, a project based on the US Federal Reserve's Beige Book –

formally the "Summary of Commentary on Current Economic Conditions" - breaks down China's economy by region and economic sector, relying on measures and qualitative assessments of economists, bankers and other experts.

Yet even the China Beige Book is oriented toward divining GDP growth; it is released before each quarterly government announcement of official statistics on economic growth, manufacturing, and inflation. If China were to really re-think its data, what if GDP were not the starting point?

Part *Moneyball*, part *Freakonomics*, *Brave New Math* asks us to rethink the economic statistics that have guided us for so long. Peter Marber points out the irony that despite supposedly living in the Information Age, the gaps in our data ecosystem are astonishing. He's modest enough not to claim to have all the answers - but he is asking the right questions: at times, looking at ways in which we should be more global in taking measurement, and at others when we should drill down to the city and regional level. Just as asking why we measure what we do is a step in the right direction, measuring more mindfully is the foundation we need to some up with better policies and predictions. In the era of Big Data, as more and more information becomes available more quickly and the technology to analyze it and identify patterns that might not even occur to us, surely we can do better at reading the numbers.

Brave New Math explores not only some of the flaws in GDP, but also in inflation, trade, productivity and unemployment. It also probes alternative statistics and contemplates what different data might mean for the United States and countries around the world as they devise future policies on education, health, taxes, defense, agriculture, workforce, cities, immigration, health, energy, innovation, housing, social security, and even on information itself.

What if, instead of being glued to their screens waiting for regular reports of Gross Domestic Product, traders fixated on another number – or set of numbers? What if they looked at a ratio of productive to destructive consumption – i.e. how much money spent on education and preventive health care versus money spent on guns and junk food? The relationship of money spent fixing messes to investment in the future?

And what if, along with those short-term measures, economists, Wall Street and policy makers paid more attention to numbers more indicative of a country's longer-term health? It's worth paying attention to trends in countries' GINI coefficients measuring income distribution and world rankings under PISA (Program for International Student Assessment) that tests 15 year-olds on mastery of key subjects. Though it starts with –you guessed it—GDP, the World Economic Forum's Global Competitiveness Report goes far beyond to cover important indicators from infrastructure quality to health and primary education to innovation.

Imagine a whole new schedule of data releases to drive countries and the markets. Sure, we can still look at the regular of menu jobless claims, trade balance, construction, inflation, home sales, personal income and outlays, manufacturing numbers, and even good/bad old GDP. But there are other data worth examining and there will be even more in the near future, creating a broader basis for policy debate and decisions. After all, we are living in the Information Age. That's what *Brave New Math* reminds us.

—Michele Wucker
World Policy Institute
January 2014

Introduction

In 1968, at age 56, my father's father had a heart attack. It surprised a lot of people. With a full head of hair, my grandfather was thin, youthful looking, and rarely sick. He received standard patient treatment for the time—prolonged bed rest and morphine. When he recovered, he continued his pre-attack lifestyle, which included smoking, almost no exercise, and a diet of meat, potatoes, and my grandmother's famous cream pastries. Five years later he was dead, the result of another heart attack.

Had my grandfather been born a quarter century later, he surely would have lived longer than 61 years. Scientific advances in the last four decades have dramatically improved the prevention, diagnosis, and treatment of heart disease. In the 1960s, the chance of dying within days of a heart attack was almost 40% in America. By the 1970s, it dropped to 25%, and in the 90s, it fell to under 10%. Today, it's about 6%. Medicine has advanced to provide us with early detection of heart disease, statins that reduce bad cholesterol, advanced coronary angiography to diagnose potential blockages, and reliable bypass surgery. We know that diet, exercise, and healthy lifestyle choices can also reduce heart disease risks, and new research continues to improve prevention and treatments. In the future, advances in nanotechnology will gather data, diagnose, and even begin to repair unhealthy parts of our bodies on a daily basis. In fact, advanced genetics research and treatments could eventually eradicate what we traditionally call "heart disease."

In some respects, the fields of medicine and economics have much in common. Both are multidisciplinary, striving to improve and maintain the health of complex systems. But unlike medicine, economics hasn't progressed much in the last 40 years. This book will examine that lack of progress.

In late 2008, the United States and many other countries suffered a major economic heart attack that might have been prevented by better diagnostics. Since then, recovery across the globe has been tepid, and many economies still face the threat of relapse. The reason so much of the world is still on life support is that governments have simply been prescribing the equivalent of economic bed rest and morphine (low interest rates and some fiscal stimulus) without any significant lifestyle changes, and measuring economic health with crude, outmoded metrics.

Traditional measures like Gross Domestic Product (GDP, or its many variants) often point to a U.S. economy that's up even when Americans are feeling down. In Europe and Japan, as well as many emerging markets, there is a similar sense of confusion over current economic directions—a universal suspicion that the numbers that have been our staples are increasingly meaningless to everyday people. These outmoded statistics skew perceptions, leaving us with a distorted worldview and a shaky foundation as a base for policy. Aren't new sets of statistical indicators available to more accurately monitor economic health? Can't we prescribe more sophisticated treatments? Are there no fresh policies to help diagnose and treat these chronic fiscal ailments? If we can't accurately diagnose the problem, how can we attempt to cure it or prevent similar problems in the future?

At the end of my last book, *Seeing the Elephant*, I explored the GDP obsession in America and worldwide, and how it often obscures more important economic phenomena. I submitted the manuscript weeks before Lehman Brothers defaulted and a merry-go-round of crisis-christening crippled the global economy. The "Subprime Crisis" became the "Credit Crunch," which was followed by the "Banking Crisis," which turned into what people feared was the "New Depression," called the "Great Recession," the "Great Slowdown," the "Global Financial Crisis," and its more recent regional variation, the "Eurozone Crisis." As a Wall Streeter who had been focused on emerging markets for nearly 25 years, I had witnessed numerous financial crises, panics, and meltdowns—as well as rebounds—so I casually grouped this one with many others I'd seen. At that time, I failed to realize that what I had written in my book might have had been related to the unfolding crisis.

Numerous books have been written in recent years to explain what has happened to America's economy. Some attack greedy bankers and poor regulation. Others, written by Wall Street insiders, officials, and academics, defend the financial industry and public policies. Libertarian writers argue that too much government wrecked the economy, while progressives insist that not enough regulation was the cause.

While there is no shortage of theories, these disparate views all share one thing: they're based on forms of statistical evidence that are, in many ways, seriously flawed. Moreover, many miss the whole point of economics: improving the human condition. The role of flawed information and poor inference in shaping policy decisions—and, therefore, in shaping economic and social behavior—lies at the heart of my own two-cent theory on the root cause of the prolonged economic malaise and related problems, including inequality, over-indebtedness, declining global competitiveness, and poor job creation. For without sound data, it's difficult to craft evidence-based policies to achieve those sound economic objectives.

I freely admit that I, too, base many of my arguments on data that could be questionable. I have little choice: economic measurements have simply not kept pace with our ever-changing global economy. And that is, perhaps, why so few "experts" saw this crisis-reset-stagnation-meltdown-depression-recession coming. The economy in the mid-2000s revealed a healthy exterior, with growing headline GDP and employment. But like my grandfather at age 56, the economy merely *appeared* healthy, and that healthy exterior masked serious disease that had grown undetected for decades.

Of the many good books written about the crisis, my two favorites are not directly about it yet shed a bright light on our economic malaise: Michael Lewis's *Moneyball* and Stephen Dubner and Steven Levitt's *Freakonomics*. *Moneyball* is an ingenious story that explains how conventional methods of managing professional baseball teams are inferior to using *sabermetrics,* a data-driven philosophy that unlocks statistically proven attributes that help teams win more ball games for less money. *Freakonomic*s, meanwhile, showcases the unintended consequences of incentive structures, reminding us that public policies are carrots and sticks that shape the way we live, work, and consume. Together, the two books help us understand what has happened in America for the last 70 years, how we've been fixating on the wrong information and organizing the wrong incentives for citizens, businesses, and politicians to create the economy that we're all grappling with today.

As *Freakonomics* reminds us, politicians have their own incentives, too—winning elections. Rising headline GDP and job creation tend to get votes. Few politicians win elections by promising to shrink the economy and reduce employment. Politicians are happy to have the front-page numbers look good, even when the underlying data look weak. Indeed, that's precisely what happened from the early 1990s through 2007. Headline GDP expanded, and headline unemployment levels were relatively low. The incentive structures *appeared* to be working. But most of us were unaware that the health of our economy was eroding relative to growing competition worldwide.

Just like the baseball managers in *Moneyball,* by failing to look behind the headline numbers, economists failed to see what was really happening. Consumer spending, fueled by credit cards, home equity loans, and government deficit spending, was too big a slice of GDP. Since the 1980s, the U.S. has been steadily replacing unionized manufacturing jobs with dead end, lower-paying, lower-skilled work that lacks security. Instead of creating a broad distribution of economic gains within the country, America has crafted incentives that benefit a tiny sliver of the population, increasing wealth inequality and disparity as a result. This steady transformation has occurred while *billions* of educated workers from emerging markets have been entering the global economy—workers who until recently were in closed, centrally planned economies. As a result, the U.S. has unleashed economic, financial, and, ultimately, *psychological* instability. Instability no one predicted. Instability America is still struggling to eliminate. And this instability is exacerbated by America's growing inequality, a phenomenon that is spreading globally.

The problems that we face are, without a doubt, enormously complex; globalization has made them so. There are more inter-linkages in life than ever before, some of which may be beyond our ability to truly comprehend. Think of the differences between playing checkers and playing chess. Both use the same board of eight by eight squares, but chess is clearly more complicated. Checkers allocates 12 identical pieces per player, each with relatively limited ability to move around the board. Chess, in contrast, assigns 16 pieces, including many that move in unique patterns. Yes, both require an ability to think ahead and to understand the future consequences of both your own and your opponent's moves. But while many of us master checkers as a child, the best chess players are the rare individuals who can think dozens of moves ahead.

If we think of the pre-industrialized world as a game of checkers, and the industrial world as chess, our brave new post-industrial world is exponentially more complex. Imagine playing chess on a board of 100 by 100 squares, and instead of starting with 16 pieces with unique limited movements, we start with 200 pieces. Imagine also that the board is three-dimensional—akin to three chessboards stacked atop each other—and moves on one-dimensional plane also affect the positioning on the other two dimensions. Few humans, if any, could play such a game. We'd need a supercomputer to calculate all the possibilities and make decisions accordingly. Humans have been ahead of machines for most of history, but in 1997 IBM's Deep Blue beat grandmaster chess champion Gary Kasparov. We now live in a time when machines can grab, calculate, and process information better and faster than any human can, and this will only accelerate in the future. In our post-industrial, rapidly globalizing world, a common man's mastery of checkers is no longer sufficient to stay on top of the game.

This is what we need to consider when crafting economic and other public policies in the 21st century. We live in a world of 3D 100x100 chessboards. With each policy move, there are winners and losers at home and abroad. We must therefore consider how each decision affects not only our only country but also climate change, cross-border terrorism and security, global supply chains, and entangled financial markets on a planet of seven billion humans. Yet our humble abilities to process and understand these phenomena—as well as our public policies to address such a changing game—have not kept pace. Unable to adapt quickly enough, we find ourselves in a much more complex world than the one my grandfather knew. Though this drastically different world is better in many respects, it will only change more as the Information Age accelerates.

We are moving into a new era, away from human hunches based on some small samples of data, toward a world that gathers and analyzes more information faster than we can imagine. Some have called information the new oil, the energy that will fuel our economy for the next few decades. While the private sector has been the first to latch onto this development known as "Big Data," it is imperative for government to master information technology to guide our economy with sound, evidence-based policies.

Public policy matters—and government needs to shepherd us through this brave new data-driven world. As I've observed in emerging markets since the late 1980s, the difference between successful and less successful countries is nothing more than decades of sound policies. Canada and Venezuela, for instance, have about the same population and export about the same amount of oil every day. But Canadians are roughly six or seven times richer than Venezuelans and enjoy more than seven additional years of life expectancy. Why? Because Canada has a long history of sound public policy. And while culture may also shape economic success, I'd still bet more on public policy. Look at the Korean peninsula. Sixty-odd years ago, the country was divided in two: The North adopted a closed Communist-style mix of policies, while the South chose an educate-export-integrate model. Two generations later, the South is roughly 17 times richer per capita than the North, and, on average, South Koreans live a remarkable 10 years longer. In addition, South Korea boasts the highest percentage of college graduates in the world. Sound policy explains why countries like Singapore, Israel, or Taiwan—countries with few natural resources—improve their people's lives. America, too, will need to keep this in mind. Cultivating human capital and building capacities is a race with no finish line.

As the complexity of modern existence has exploded exponentially, it has ushered in great benefits as well as great confusion. We have at our disposal new ways to gather and analyze data, as well as many new indicators. Venturing forth in this brave new world will require shedding conventional wisdom about economics and crafting better public policies around globalization and information. Rather than fearing the complex phenomena engulfing us, we must harness it.

I'm optimistic. Americans are resilient and adaptable, and signs suggest we've already begun to reshape the ways we think and live. But we should not relax just because stock markets hit record levels and headline GDP and unemployment rates improve. To guard against future collapses a build a stronger future, we must understand flaws in our statistics, develop a better information infrastructure, and explore new goals and public policies around a broader set of data.

PM
Boston, Massachusetts
December 2013

I
Globalization, Information, and Measuring Our Brave New World

"Information is not knowledge."
—Albert Einstein

Crescat scientia; vito excolatur.
"Let knowledge grow from more to more;
and so be human life enriched."
—Unknown

"You don't measure the right thing,
you don't do the right thing."
—Joseph Stiglitz

"Stupid is as stupid does."
—Forrest Gump

In June 2009 it became official: America's longest economic recession since World War II was over. It had lasted 18 months.

Economic recession in the postwar period has typically been defined as two consecutive negative quarters of Gross Domestic Production (GDP) .[1] Today, years later, many Americans probably feel that they're still in some kind of recession, regardless of the word's technical definition.

Newspapers, radio, and television routinely spout headlines listing key statistics on GDP, inflation, and employment. These astonishingly influential indicators are computed—often manually and on tiny relative budgets—in the United States by the Bureau of Labor

---

[1] While the discussion herein is limited to GDP, it's also applicable to related concepts such as Gross National Product (GNP) and Gross National Income (GNI).

Statistics (BLS) and Bureau of Economic Analysis (BEA), and in capitals around the world by comparable agencies. Governments, businesses, and individuals consistently use these yardsticks in their decision-making, and even minor data revisions can have major ramifications. Inflation measurements, for example, help determine mortgage and savings rates; stock market prices; interest payments on the national debt; and cost-of-living increases for wages, pensions, and Social Security benefits. But in the 21st century, these indicators often have little correlation with the realities on the street, Wall or Main.

Overwhelmingly, the numbers that are trumpeted in today's media are "noise," as statisticians say, not the "signal." They are conventional measurements unable to fully capture the complexity of our 21st century economy. In fact, the world of today is so fundamentally different from that of 30 or 40 years ago that the methods we commonly use to understand the state of the economy perform no more predictably than a divining rod in search of water. Two revolutionary forces—globalization and information—have transformed modern life in ways our species could not have comprehended just a few generations ago. And as a result, our tools, metrics, and philosophies used to understand this brave new world need a serious upgrade.

In the entertaining opening scene of *Moneyball*, the 2011 film based on Michael Lewis's book by the same name, gray-haired insiders are evaluating several young ballplayers. "He's got a baseball body," one says. "He can't hit a curveball," another notes. One prospect's ugly girlfriend is chalked up to a lack of confidence. In the old world of baseball, such subjective eyeballing formed the basis of evaluating talent. Even after newer, more scientific methods of evaluating talent had been discovered, many talent scouts stuck with the old techniques. Psychologists call this resistance to new information that doesn't agree with our preconceived conclusions "affirmation bias."

Challenging a century of baseball dogma, statistician Bill James developed "sabermetrics," which showed that certain statistics, such as on-base percentage, were more useful than conventional observations in predicting wins. Accordingly, many overlooked players who lacked a "baseball body" were actually more productive when evaluated according to their slugging percentage and on-base percentage, as opposed to traditional metrics like batting average or stolen bases. After all, runs win ballgames. More importantly, at least from an owner's perspective, the overlooked players' salaries were cheap compared to those of sexy superstars with supermodel girlfriends. As shown in *Moneyball*, James's data-driven philosophy helped the 2002 Oakland A's win as many games as the New York Yankees—with less than one-third of the salary budget. Bill James is what I'd call one of the first brave new mathematicians of our time.

When evaluating our economy, are we like old baseball scouts, looking at headline GDP, unemployment, and inflation just because that's what we've always done? Can the *Moneyball* approach somehow be applied to economics and public policy? Today, when it comes to evaluating the national and world economy, we have more data points than ever before. Yet raw data aren't worth much without proper analysis. And the way we've been analyzing our economy—relying on traditional blunt measurements like GDP, unemployment, and inflation—is outmoded and flawed. The few indicators that we pick out of the vast sea of data no longer tell us what we need to know in order to measure, diagnose, and direct our economy. Needless to say, such an affirmation bias is wholly avoidable in the Information Age.

The Information Revolution

Anyone born in the last 50 years has lived through an unprecedented information revolution, which will continue to reshape the way we live as well as think about the world. From the beginning of recorded time until 2003, humanity created only five exabytes of data—the equivalent of five *billion* gigabytes. But in the last decade there has been a quantum leap: by 2011, our world was generating that amount in two days, and by the time you read this, we might be creating five exabytes every five or 10 minutes.

Information, available in nearly unlimited quantities, dominates virtually every aspect of 21st century existence. From newspapers to TV, from the telephone to the Internet, information is the life-blood of modernity. If you don't believe me, try going a day or two without it. You'll likely feel disoriented, anxious even—the same way you'd feel if you hadn't slept or eaten. Information grounds our existence. It offers points of reference for comparison. It frees us from ignorance by exposing untruths and superstitions.

And there is more to come. We are on the cusp of an information flood, which will in turn lead to the availability of "meta-information," information about our information. Indeed, almost everything today—music, video, telephone calls—can be broken down, digitized, and turned into information. Every text, every email, every voice conversation on a cell phone, every posted picture and YouTube video, and every image on a surveillance camera is converted into digital information. In time, there will be sensors and systems that capture even more, from how much carbon dioxide trees absorb to how much ocean temperatures fluctuate, from how fast traffic is moving to how many *Big Gulps* of Diet Coke are being consumed. In the near future, almost every piece of data that can be captured *will be.*

Even today, we are living in an era of the "Internet of Things." From railroads to pacemakers, countless physical objects are embedded with sensors and devices. The sensors and devices in turn, are linked through wired and wireless networks connected to the Internet. These modern networks can and will churn out huge volumes of data that flow to supercomputers for analysis. When objects can both sense the environment and communicate, they become tools for understanding complexity, tools with an unprecedented ability to respond swiftly. What's truly amazing about this revolution is that it's quietly being deployed already, often working without human intervention. The technology is set to accelerate further with "exascale computing," computers able to perform one billion *billion* calculations per second—1,000 times faster than computers process information today. This new megatrend, often called "Big Data," really is big. Coupled with faster computing, Big Data has the potential to act like global X-rays, allowing us to see things in places that had previously been invisible to the naked eye.

But as Richard Saul Wurman, founder of the TED conference series, warned presciently in 1989 before the widespread adoption of the Internet, the increased volume of information is not valuable in and of itself. With too much information and no good way to filter it, we often fall into what he called, "the black hole between data and knowledge," a place where, "information doesn't tell us what we want or need to know." Before the Information Age, which we might say began in the late 1970s and followed with the introduction of the personal computer, data required manual collection. As someone who has worked in universities for more than 20 years, I have seen academia evolve from a culture of data "hunters and gatherers" to data "analyzers" like the baseball statistician Bill James. This is a profound change, one that is not fully appreciated by young academics. Any professor who used to rely on typewriters, telephones, national postal systems, library card catalogs, books, and physical travel can attest to how much the discipline has been changed by computers and software, the Internet and search engines, e-mail and video-chat. With new information technology, the goals of academia have shifted to probing data; identifying patterns, structures, and relationships; analyzing causes and effects; and forecasting.

Information's importance, particularly in a democracy, extends far beyond universities or baseball stadiums. Information is evidence, evidence we need to craft sound, efficient public policies. Without evidence, our ideas, opinions, and speculations are just that: ideas, opinions, and speculations, which are fine for cocktail party conversations but not for running a country. Our Information Age can scientifically ground decision-making, thereby turning ideas, opinions, and speculation into validated reality. The scientific method— beginning with a question, constructing a hypothesis, and testing that hypothesis—requires us to test our hunches and theories against the available evidence. It's an arduous process that involves trial and error, but when our theories match the evidence—i.e., when our ideas reflect empirical reality—we find a great deal of reassurance.

Proven theories have a predictive quality, which is crucial to policy formulation. If this process doesn't tell us what we should expect to observe, or if the predictions are vague and general (think about fortune cookies, psychic readings, or horoscopes), then the theories— and policies—are worthless. Properly mastered, analyzing and understanding information helps create *knowledge*. In this respect, information can help us navigate the complex, modern world of the 21st century, a world in which inter-linkages, as we've discussed, have never been greater.

Harnessing Big Data will give us the ability to sort through masses of newly gathered information, finding hidden patterns correlations and, perhaps, some surprise connections. It's already being used in big business, where retailers like Amazon provide customized recommendations for us. Media firms, meanwhile, can accurately target advertising instead of relying on the old method of blanketing broad populations in their campaigns. And in politics, Nate Silver analyzed millions of pieces of voting behavior data and correctly predicted nearly 100% of the state Electoral College winners for the 2008 and 2012 U.S. presidential elections. Silver has also built models to successfully predict outcomes of baseball and soccer games.

We're also seeing data and connectivity in ways that can truly help improve well-being. Google's Flu Trends service, for example, uses online search queries related to flu-like symptoms, often discovering increases in flu cases *weeks* in advance of Centers for Disease Control and Prevention (CDC) records. This data can help limit and contain outbreaks. Digitizing medical records is already helping identify potential genealogical risks, finding the statistically most effective treatments for certain diseases, better pinpointing drug interactions, matching blood and organ donors faster, and saving lives and billions of dollars in wasted tests and misdiagnoses.

Global farming is harnessing information to help feed the world's growing population, which will swell by an extra two billion by 2050. In a trend that should double per-acre yields by 2030, Big Data is reshaping seed planting and fertilization practices by helping farmers buy localized weather insurance and track atmospheric changes and weather patterns more precisely. One company, the Climate Corporation, already provides such insurance policies for up to two years by analyzing weather, soil, and crop yield data and running trillions of simulations to determine predicative values.

As cheap information technology becomes ubiquitous, so-called crowdsourcing is uniting thousands of scientists and amateurs to help solve problems in everything from astronomy to zoology. Research is often quite labor intensive, with scientists spending countless hours peering through microscopes and manually analyzing cells. In an effort to better allocate time and resources, lab professionals are taking untrained people from all over the world—people whose scientific training hardly extends beyond high school biology—and turning them into image analysts, getting results comparable to those of professionals. Harvard University's Tuberculosis Lab, for example, has used crowdsourcing to count neurons, an activity that computer vision can't yet solve. In addition to expediting the image review process, crowdsourcing has freed the Harvard lab team to do more advanced levels of research and analysis.

Gathering more information and evidence can help improve decision-making and help formulate action plans to reshape the world. Nevertheless, in the age of Microsoft, Apple, and Google, our governments too often operate with the equivalent of carbon paper and an adding machine. Public policy not grounded in evidence-based data is reckless—and potentially expensive.

Globalization

Globalization, one of the major offshoots of our information boom, can be understood as the holistic outcome of four powerful laws that feed off each other. The first law, Moore's Law, notes that computers become faster and cheaper as microprocessor speed doubles every 18 months. The second, Gilder's Law, observes that the total bandwidth of communication systems triples every 12 months. The third, Metcalfe's Law, reveals that as a network grows, the value of being connected to it grows exponentially. These first three laws have helped wire and connect our planet with billions of phones, computers, and tablets. Fourth and finally, there's the important but lesser known Wriston's Law, named after the late Citigroup Chairman Walter Wriston, who predicted the rise of electronic networks and their ripple effects. Wriston famously quipped that "capital will always go where it's welcome and stay where it's well treated. . . . Capital is not just money. It's also talent and ideas. They, too, will go where they're welcome and stay where they are well treated." The flow of capital, which began only in the last generation, has occurred at an astonishing rate.

In 1970, world output was roughly 20% of what it was in 2012, with only modest trade. The world of the early 1970s consisted of a patchwork of inward-focused economies, each of which relied on domestically manufactured and sold goods. Very little cross-border trade in finished products existed, and what did exist occurred between only 20 or 30 "First World" countries. Countries like China and the former Soviet Union, which operated under a communist or socialist model, were closed off from trade. Even in the United States, trade comprised less than 1/7 of economic activity.

The widespread abandonment of socialist and isolationist policies since the mid-1980s in favor of global trade and investment—plus the adoption of new information technologies—has ushered in the first truly global era in which goods, services, capital, talent, and ideas move across borders faster than ever before. While Wriston's Law has played out on a global scale, the world economy has been transformed into a complex system of interdependent and constantly changing relationships. No longer a patchwork quilt, the global economy today is an interwoven tapestry. And just when you think you understand the tapestry's pattern, it begins to unwind and form a new tapestry, reflecting the rate of change in global supply chains and financial markets that now include more than 100 countries. Global production and distribution chains mesh Brazilian iron mines, Greek ships, Chinese steelmakers, German automakers, Wall Street banks, and car dealers in Peoria. Financial markets instantly entangle California pension funds, insurers in Asia, and Cayman Island hedge funds with banks everywhere. Today's official global economy amounts to more than $70 trillion dollars, with roughly 25% in trade.

Oddly, globalization and information might have received their biggest boost during the Asian financial crisis of 1997-1998, a period when many thought globalization was about to die. During the last months of 1997, the World Trade Organization (WTO) helped formalize the Information Technology Agreement (ITA), which reduced tariffs on computing and related components to zero.[2] This included everything from disk drives to microprocessors to calculators to flat screen monitors. Eliminating such taxes gave birth to our

---

[2] A special thanks to Michael Mandel for highlighting this important and often overlooked fact.

modern supply chains, allowing multinational corporations to begin complex "offshoring," with components made in several countries and assembled elsewhere. Such a development represented comparative advantage and free trade in almost their purest forms, and as a result the information technology business grew from just over $1.2 trillion in 1998 to an estimated $7 trillion—almost 10% of the world's economic activity. But more importantly, it helped drive down tech component costs, spurring world trade, creating economic organizations, and spawning our gadget-driven Information Age.

Information and globalization mean more ideas, goods, money, and people flow across borders. With a population of seven billion and growing, the earth has more literate, healthy, productive humans than ever before in history, and our ability to shape our own destiny—for better or worse—has been mushrooming for decades. The capacity to control food supply and to rid ourselves of diseases that have plagued humans for eons has given us greater control over our species. Couple information technology, including electronic money movement and financial markets, with advances in transportation like aviation and intermodal shipping, and we have a global economy that could never have been imagined by Adam Smith or David Ricardo two centuries ago—or even by John Maynard Keynes in the 1930s. Today's world befuddles most ordinary citizens as well as many trained economists and government officials. What will happen within a generation when almost *everyone* and *everything* is linked globally to *everyone* and *everything else everywhere?* Are we preparing for this brave new world?

We are just on the cusp of controlling information and globalization. Nowhere is this more evident than in the social science of economics. Economics is not necessarily a single discipline but a unique field that overlaps with political science, demography, natural sciences, sociology, and psychology, among others. It's a field that has gained particular prominence in the realm of government and policy formulation in the last few decades. Unfortunately, economists are playing catch-up with the explosion of information and globalization and have not managed in the last several decades to make any significant changes to the way we measure an economy. As a result, most policies today are based on sketchy, incomplete information and guesswork. As with the baseball saga *Moneyball*, conventional approaches need to be modernized. Just as truths that we believed centuries ago have been disproved—like the sun revolving around the earth—surely there are commonly followed economic principles and policies that are destined to be delegitimized in the very near future.

The Obsession with GDP

No single metric has changed how we look at public policy more than Gross Domestic Product. GDP has its origins in the 1930s, when Congress asked young University of Pennsylvania economist Simon Kuznets to develop a uniform set of national accounts to help officials grasp Depression-era economic realities. Economist Richard Froyen explains the scarcity of good data before GDP: "Presidents Hoover and then Roosevelt design[ed] policies to combat the Great Depression of the 1930s on the basis of such sketchy data as stock price indices, freight car loadings, and incomplete indices of industrial production." Kuznets's new measure proved to be a watershed development because it provided greater clarity than ever before. In fact, more than 60 years later, the U.S. Department of Commerce lauded the development of GDP as "its achievement of the century." GDP's genius lay with its simplicity. It gave a single standardized and easily comparable figure for the total market value of all final goods and services produced within a country's economic territory during a given period. While not perfect, it was more accurate than the measures that predated it.

By examining components of the national economy—consumption (C), government spending (G), investment (I), and net exports (NX)—analysts now had a more rigorous way to assess the impact of different tax and spending plans, the impact of price shocks, and the impact of monetary policy on the economy. Armed with this new, powerful tool, economists were able to better manage the wartime economy, and they ultimately became the central policy authorities of the postwar era. It worked for a few decades in the 20th century, helping raise living standards after the war. There's also some evidence that GDP has been useful for government to smooth out economic volatility. Two professors at the University of Illinois have reconstructed GDP data prior to its introduction and found that official recessions were far more common *before* it was introduced in 1933. In fact, from the Panic of 1873, often considered the first Great Depression, to 1933, the U.S. weathered recessions 52% of the time. Since 1933, the U.S. has only endured recessions 16% of the time.

The idea of national accounting was hardly new. In 1665, well before Adam Smith's famous *Wealth of Nations*, Englishman William Petty tried to scientifically gauge a country's size and economic health. Petty, Cromwell's chief economist and a secretary to political philosopher Thomas Hobbes, was one of the first thinkers to note that a country's wealth was larger than just its gold and silver. In attempting to measure the value of the British economy, Petty discovered that England's stock market was worth more than all its physical assets. He attributed the difference to the "value of people," that is, to human capital. This observation, made almost 350 years ago, provides a clue as to how governments should utilize economic statistics in the 21st century.

While GDP's ease-of-use may still be attractive, its status as a national obsession is not. Coupled with the official unemployment rate, it has become one of two metrics by which a country's economy is often judged, creating a ripple effect. But the two stats alone are hardly enough to make good policy or shape good behavior. And GDP as a benchmark simply hasn't kept up with the increasingly globalized and increasingly complicated modern economy.

Bill Cobb, Herman Daly, and Ted Halstead, the founders of the think tank Redefining Progress, noted in 1995 that economic indicators like GDP define the economic problems that the political arena seeks to address. "If the nation's indicators of economic progress are obsolete," they pointed out, "then they consign us to continually resorting to policies that cannot succeed because they aren't addressing the right problems." Worse yet, an outmoded indicator—and incentives to boost that indicator—can create new problems. As Steven Levitt and Stephen Dubner pointed out in their entertaining and insightful *Freakonomics*, incentives can drive behavior in ways that are not immediately obvious—or desirable.

The overreliance on GDP as a measure of a politician's performance creates a strong incentive for governments to monkey with statistics. Perceived economic progress can boost an incumbent political party's chances of staying in power. In my last book, *Seeing the Elephant,* I cited the example of Greece massaging GDP estimates to gain entry into the European Monetary Union – which has turned into one of Europe's worst headaches.

GDP's accuracy is dubious for more benign reasons, as well. Economic policy advisers often propose policies based on adjustments in national income of *fractions of a percent*—statistically insignificant shifts. Back in 1950, economist Oskar Morgenstern noted that our ability to measure national income had a 10% margin for error, making such fractional movements questionable.

On a more fundamental level, many countries lack computing infrastructure and adequately trained professionals capable of observing economic data in a timely fashion; they often compile small samples by hand and make estimates. But these manual estimates cannot keep pace with rapidly changing economies. Such data is still prone to error, and varying national standards make cross-border comparisons difficult. To be fair, no indicator can ever be completely free of intentional manipulation and poor data collection. Nevertheless, critical policy decisions are made every day on the basis of GDP growth, with little accounting for a wide margin of error. And we know the data are often wrong; there are data revisions as often as there are data releases.

It's possible that some of the key statistics that we use regularly have become "golden instruments," falling victim to what some call Goodhart's Law. Attributed to a Bank of England adviser in the 1970s, the law states that, as soon as an indicator is relied upon for policy decisions, it stops being effective. For example, police can reduce the rate of shoplifting by shifting more resources from other crime-fighting activities. Shoplifting rates go down, but other crime rates go up. As a result, shoplifting becomes a useless indicator of overall crime trends. In this respect, when a particular yardstick like GDP is used as a performance indicator of a complex system—such as a national economy—the government might choose to target the measure, improving its value but at other costs to the country. As such, GDP might improve, but it becomes less useful as a measure of the broader economy and national well-being. In other instances, indicators such as inflation and unemployment have been hijacked and don't actually mean what we once thought they did. When the measures we use to describe our economy and our everyday life don't have objective or consistent meaning, it begins to feel a little like Orwell's *Nineteen Eighty-Four*, that we're being told that things are okay when they're not, like two plus two equals five.

But perhaps the biggest problem is when policymakers "teach to the test." Just like a grade school teacher who focuses on standardized test scores to the detriment of real learning, policymakers' dogged focus on GDP has created perverse incentives and unhealthy imbalances in the U.S. economy. This is Goodhart's Law at work. Look at the recent financial crisis. For decades, government and the broader country set targets to expand the GDP and to lower unemployment and formulated policy and incentives accordingly. GDP growth and low unemployment are exactly what we got in the short-term—and maybe in the long-term, too. But the *quality* of that GDP and employment growth was ambiguous at best.

Quantity vs. Quality

Let's be clear on what GDP can and cannot do. GDP measures goods and services exchanged in the formal economy. It does not, however, measure human well-being or happiness. GDP is often used as a proxy indicator of these more difficult-to-measure concepts, yet even its creator acknowledged this was beyond GDP's scope. In 1934, Kuznets warned, "the welfare of a nation can scarcely be inferred from measurement of national income." Over time, that warning has been widely forgotten.

GDP is defined as the monetary value of all the finished goods and services produced within a country, calculated on an annual basis in the following simple economic equation:

$$GDP = C + G + I + NX \text{ where:}$$

"**C**" is equal to all private consumption, or consumer spending, in the economy,
"**G**" is the sum of government spending,

"**I**" is investment, the sum of all the country's businesses spending on capital,
"**NX**" is the nation's total net exports, calculated as total exports minus total imports.

We can see that GDP is really a *quantity* measurement of formal economic activity, of velocity, with few details on the *quality* of such activity. The indicator cannot answer such essential questions as whether we are consuming too much of the wrong things, exporting the right things, or saving enough. To any government statistician tallying GDP, $100 spent on textbooks is no more valuable to society than $100 spent on junk food. Americans spend more than $150 billion on junk food each year and more than $150 billion on the health care costs related to obesity-linked illnesses. Together that's about 2% of American GDP—nothing to boast about.

Since GDP includes all activities in which money changes hands, it does not distinguish between productive uses of cash and so-called "regrettables" or "bads," such as spending on crime and disaster remediation. GDP is unable to capture the fact that victims of floods, hurricanes, wildfires, and earthquakes are merely replacing destroyed property, not adding to their wealth or happiness. Going to the hospital and receiving chemotherapy adds oodles to GDP.

On the flipside, GDP also fails to capture some economic activity, both constructive and destructive. It excludes the value of non-market goods and services, such as natural resources, not to mention informal and unpaid activities. If your mother stays at home, for example, and cooks and cleans, her effort isn't reported in GDP. But if she works at an office, sends clothes to a laundry and dry cleaning service, and takes your family out to dinner a couple times a week, America gets a GDP boost every time the cash register rings. Unreported, non-monetized activities have become an increasingly important, yet unmeasured, segment of the economy, particularly during a recession, when people do repairs themselves more often or bargain hunt for used items. Ever buy or sell something used in the Pennysaver, on eBay, or at a flea market? If you have, there's a good chance this wasn't captured in GDP. Buying a TV on Craigslist, for example, puts money into the pocket of a seller (a good thing), and the buyer gets a good deal, too. Who loses? Stores like Best Buy and the formal GDP.

In today's globalized world, understanding the quality of GDP and its composition, especially the weighting of its four constituent parts, is increasingly important to a country's long-term national health. Roughly 70% of U.S. GDP falls under "C," personal consumption expenditures. In a study for the Federal Reserve Bank of St. Louis, William Emmons noted in the chart below that, since 1980, the U.S. has seen a steady rise in personal consumption from roughly 62.5% to 70% of GDP, a small decline in government spending, a modest decline in investment, and a disturbing fall in net exports to -4.5%, which has meant *a rise in net imports*. If we lump some of this 4.5% of imports in with personal consumption (because Americans are consuming imports like oil for their SUVs and new flat-screen TVs made in China), we can see that, for a generation now, Americans have been using credit cards and second mortgages to spend like drunken sailors. Television news programs often report that consumers drive two-thirds of the U.S. economy. Does it have to be this way?

Actually the national composition of C, G, I, and NX varies from country to country. If we look to Canada, America's neighbor to the north, we see a moderately different GDP mix, with considerably less consumer spending, higher levels of investment, a positive trade balance, and more government spending. And if we think the U.S. has a better economy than Canada, note that in life expectancy, one of the better barometers of success, the average Canadian lives about three years longer than the average American—a huge bio-social difference.

Canada's more stable GDP mix could explain why it didn't suffer nearly as much as the U.S. during the recent slowdown. Canada's slightly higher spending on government/human capital could also explain why it's a few places ahead of the U.S. in the World Bank's Knowledge Economy Index, where it moved from 10th to 7th place from 2000 to 2012, while America fell eight places to number 12.

Peter Marber

Figure 1.

Composition of GDP in the U.S. and Canada, 1961-2010

U.S.

Average annual share of GDP (percent)	Consumer Expenditure	Investment	Net Exports	Government Expenditures
1961-70	61.8	20.5	0.6	17.1
1971-80	62.5	20.6	-0.3	17.2
1981-90	64.6	20.3	-1.9	17.0
1991-2000	67.3	18.9	-1.5	15.3
2001-10	70.0	18.6	-4.5	15.9

Canada

Average annual share of GDP (percent)	Consumer Expenditure	Investment	Net Exports	Government Expenditures
1961-70	58.8	23.3	0.7	17.1
1971-80	54.4	23.8	0.5	21.2
1981-90	54.9	21.5	1.7	21.7
1991-2000	57.6	19.2	2.1	21.2
2001-10	56.4	21.4	2.4	19.8

Differences: U.S. minus Canada

Average annual share of GDP (percent)	Consumer Expenditure	Investment	Net Exports	Government Expenditures
1961-70	3	-2.8	-0.1	0.0
1971-80	8.1	-3.2	-0.7	-4.0
1981-90	9.7	-1.2	-3.6	-4.8
1991-2000	9.7	-0.2	-3.6	-5.8
2001-10	13.6	-2.8	-6.9	-3.9

Consumption itself isn't particularly bad, but much of American consumption has been driven by debt from credit cards, home equity loans, and government borrowing. A consumption-and-debt-fueled economy boosts GDP in the short run but could curb future growth when households have to pay back the debt and consume less. Government borrowing could fall into this trap as well. If the U.S. government borrows $500 billion to $1 trillion dollars annually from investors abroad by deficit spending, current GDP may appear inflated as that money circulates in the economy, but eventually servicing this debt will reduce GDP. Borrowing money pumps up the economy in the short run, but often deflates it over the longer run. This is true for households, too. In a 2009 study for the National Bureau of Economic Research, Atif Mian and Amir Sufi of the University of Chicago noted a steady rise in household debt since 1975. The rise accelerated sharply between 2002 and 2007 as additional home equity-based borrowing equaled a remarkable 2.8% of U.S. GDP *every year* from 2002 to 2006. Much of the pain of the 2007 recession was fallout from America's debt-fueled GDP-pumping exercise. In fact, America's collective national debt—public and private combined—has gone from 160% of GDP in 1980 to an alarming 355% by year-end 2012. How much of America's GDP growth has been nothing more than debt-financed C + G? Probably most of it.

Not all debt is bad. Companies generally borrow money to invest in productive assets that generate long-term value that is greater than the debt service. That's generally not what consumers and government borrowing does. An extra few hundred *billion* for defense spending, for example, generally goes toward short-term consumption versus longer-term investments. So if the government borrows $500 billion, or 3.5% of GDP, and pumps it into the economy, can we really consider that GDP expansion? If consumers take out home equity loans and fill their houses with imported goods, is this really a healthy exercise? While economists might debate the value of debt, there clearly becomes a time when the use of debt is actually bad for an economy. At a minimum, there is a point at which its use distorts the true picture of economic health.

Is there something inherently wrong with a consumer-driven economy? Not really, if you are playing the "whoever has the most GDP wins" game. As we mentioned earlier, an additional dollar of consumer spending boosts GDP just as much as a dollar of infrastructure, business investment, or exports. But like calories, some are worse for our health than others, particularly when they are extremely lopsided. Many economists find both theoretical reasons and empirical evidence to suggest U.S. long-term growth prospects may have been harmed by the *decades-long* consumer binge leading to the 2008 crash.

Standard economic growth theories from Nobel Laureate Robert Barro and others suggest that countries must continuously invest in infrastructure and capital goods in order to raise labor productivity and boost living standards over time. Countries that invest a higher percentage of income tend to grow GDP faster than those where consumer spending "crowds out" investments. Emmons telling 2012 study revealed that higher investment in America generally has been linked to lower consumer spending, and vice versa, as a percentage of official GDP. From 1951 to 2010, consumer spending was generally lower than average when investment was higher than average, and vice versa. Moreover, just as in many studies that have compared the economies of several countries, higher investment spending ("I") has been associated with higher economic growth, while years of relatively high consumer spending ("C") have been associated with relatively low GDP growth in the U.S.

America wasn't always like this. Once upon a time, it was a frugal nation. Remember Ben Franklin's adage, "a penny saved is a penny earned"? Today America's mantra is "when the going gets tough, the tough go shopping!" In her book *The Land of Too Much,* sociologist Monica Prasad chronicles America's transformation from thrifty to spendthrifty with convincing, interlocking arguments about credit, taxation, overproduction and overconsumption, regulation, American special interest politics, and inequality since the late 1800s. These changes were rooted particularly in the government response to the Depression that, Prasad argues, fostered a demand-side theory that explains key structural differences between the U.S. economy and

European economies (and the Canadian economy, which looks like a hybrid). Prasad calls the mix of policies "mortgage Keynesianism," a reference to John Maynard Keynes's notion of government spending to boost demand and smooth out the economy when the private sector weakens.

According to Prasad, America's explosive economic growth during the Industrial Revolution in the late 19th century overwhelmed world supply, causing price declines everywhere. She postulates that while European countries adopted protectionist policies in response to such "dumping," the U.S. government began decades of policies around increasing domestic credit and, thus, domestic demand. As European countries focused on investment and exports, the U.S. developed a growth model based on consumption. These large-scale U.S. government interventions led to improved living standards through private credit rather than through advances in social welfare or human capital. The most important interventions include the formation of the Federal Home Loan Banking system in 1932, the Government National Mortgage Association (GNMA or Ginnie Mae) in 1968, and the Federal Home Loan Mortgage Corporation (FHLMC, or Freddie Mac) in 1970. These institutions, plus tax policies to encourage borrowing for houses and public support for highways and roads, helped nurture what I'll call America's "Nesting Nation," an economy built on housing and personal consumption.

In essence, government created America's consumption-biased economy by ensuring plentiful access to credit to buy houses and more goods, keeping U.S. GDP humming along. That's why America's personal consumption ("C") is so high relative to that of most advanced economies, particularly European ones, and certainly compared to the economies of lesser-developed countries. But as we'll see, a Nesting Nation built on perverse incentives leads to *Freakonomic* outcomes.

Trade

Consumption is also captured in trade, the "NX" component of GDP. Trade in the U.S. has declined since the early 1970s, falling from a modest surplus of .6% in 1971 to a deficit of more than 5% by the late 2000s. How does this fit into our story? It confirms the underlying globalization that has been in making for nearly a century, a process that shaped American labor and economic trends. I've witnessed it first-hand in my family's business.

In 1929, my family began manufacturing gloves in Gloversville, New York. Glovemaking is a low-tech business, requiring a considerable amount of manual labor to cut, stretch, sew, and knit. After World War II, as industrialization swept the nation, workers left Gloversville to take jobs in factories, where they made cars, refrigerators, televisions—you name it. Those factories offered higher wages. As a result, my family shifted production to Japan and Italy, two countries that possessed abundant low-skilled labor after the war. But then wages in Europe and Japan rose in the 1950s as their people became more productive. Japan started producing electronics and cars, just like U.S. workers had a generation earlier. So glove production shifted again—this time to South Korea, Taiwan, and the Philippines— until labor grew expensive like it had in Japan, Europe, and the U.S. In the late 1980s, my dad moved production to China, trying to capitalize on that country's cheap labor, but he tells me today there are even lesser developed countries that are beginning to compete in gloves.

My family's experience in the glove-making business isn't unique and sheds light on America's economic development. After World War II, most things sold in America were made in America. But as America's labor grew more productive and its people became better educated, countless low-skilled jobs were exported to other countries, paving the way for globalization.

Globalization is a continuous process, whereby many competing countries keep improving productivity and move up the value chain. You hope that you can produce things cheaply and exchange them for other goods through comparative advantage and free trade. The system is predicated on comparative advantage theory, that one advanced country can export a $300 million airplane to a middle-income country in exchange for 10,000 cars at $30,000, or to an even lesser developed country for one million $300 TVs. Different national wage and productivity levels determine who makes what most efficiently.

Everyone specializes in their own sectors and trades, and everyone is happy. That's the theory.

Since World War II, American wages have risen as productivity has increased, and trade tariffs have been lowered by more than 90%. This has opened the door for many rising countries to produce the same things for lower cost and spur global trade. And as personal consumption has grown in America, so has the number of imports, whether TVs, cars, clothes, or commodities. Energy, in particular, has played a significant role in America's trade balance since the first oil shocks in the 1970s, but this also accelerated after 1998, when the ITA paved the wave for modern supply chains.

Unfortunately, trade is less about individual finished goods like cars and computers than it was in the past. According to the World Bank, some two-thirds of what crosses borders today are so-called "intermediate goods"—components that go into other products, like hard drives that go into computers or engine parts into automobiles. Global supply chains lead to segmented production processes across borders and create distinct challenges for measuring and understanding the economy and international interdependence.

A country's trade statistics often obfuscate the notion of whether its "tradable" economy is doing better or worse. Distortions can emerge at each step of the manufacturing or distributing process. First, conventional trade statistics count the gross dollar value of goods crossing each border, rather than the net value added. This is a common double-counting problem in which the full values of the import and the export may overstate the domestic value-added content of exports. Two excellent studies on Apple gadget production, one by the University of California at Irvine and one by the Asia Development Bank, help expose globalization's distortion of trade statistics. Say, for example, China imports $143 worth of intermediate parts for an iPod from places like Germany, Japan, South Korea, and Israel. In turn, China assembles and then exports the finished iPod to the United States for $150, after which China officially registers $150 in exports. But the value-added component of the Chinese export is only seven dollars. The finished product is then sold for $250 to $300. Isn't America's iPod trade "deficit" really less with China and more with Japan, Germany, Israel, and South Korea? If Americans are worried that China is stealing good jobs for that $7, just remember that hipsters working at Apple's Genius Bar earn that in 30-40 minutes.

Some economists estimate that the import content of exports is 15 to 20% in countries like the United States and up to 50% in heavy manufacturing countries like China. So the more expensive the imported content, the more distorted trade statistics—and overall GDP—can become. In this respect, many lower-end emerging markets are actually less of a trade threat than more advanced countries. We might think the U.S. runs a large trade imbalance with China, for example, because it runs a huge headline deficit with that country. But America's true value-added trade volume with China is probably lower than politicians would have Americans believe. When it comes to iPads and iPods, the U.S. actually may be running bigger deficits with Japan and Germany. Like GDP itself, trade is a complicated concept that hasn't been refined during globalization.

In short, these simple ingredients of GDP—C, G, I, and NX—no longer tell the whole story. So while the *quantity* of GDP has been buoyant for decades, the composition and *quality* of that GDP certainly has been suspect.

Population Distortions of GDP

Traditional measures of GDP also fail to illuminate the relationship between economic growth and population. Per capita GDP, not total GDP, can actually tell us something about the human experience. Given that the U.S. population is growing by roughly 1% a year, a GDP growth rate below that means the real per capita income is actually *contracting*. As a population grows, consumption rises and GDP generally grows. If the government reports, "GDP has expanded 1% this year," while the population has increased by 1%, per capita, GDP is actually flat. Unfortunately, Americans don't calculate population as frequently as they do GDP. This seems myopic, given that the U.S. has adequate technology to determine its population in terms of births, deaths, and immigration in real-time—and could probably do that more accurately than it calculates GDP.

So what really constitutes a recession? Is it two consecutive quarters of contracting GDP in aggregate, or per capita? If it's per capita, the U.S. has likely experienced more recessions than official government data suggests. Accordingly, if we examine a recent five-year snapshot of U.S. economic performance, our findings will vary widely, depending on which figures we use: per capita or aggregate GDP. During the boom years 2003 through 2007, for example, the popular perception was that America's dynamic economy was beating Japan's with official GDP growth of 2.9% compared to 2.1%. However, the per capita calculation paints a very different picture. America's population increased about 1% per annum during this period, while that of Japan remained fairly flat—and actually began to shrink in 2005. Therefore, adjusting for per capita (or maybe by the size of the active workforce), Japan's economy actually grew slightly faster.

By refocusing on per capita GDP, we change the whole notion of recession—officially, two quarters of consecutive national GDP contraction—and the corresponding policies to combat recession. Again, as in *Moneyball,* we're looking at the wrong statistics and making poor inferences. Stagnant total GDP in depopulating countries like Japan or Italy actually isn't so bad if official per capita GDP is still rising. But in countries with growing populations like America (and most developing countries), the average citizen might be worse off. Therefore, a better definition of recession—sticking with GDP terms—would be declining per capita income for an agreed-upon period.

Purchasing Power Parity

Have you ever travelled to another country and noticed that a cup of Starbucks coffee or a McDonalds Big Mac costs a little more or less than in your hometown? This is called "purchasing power parity" (PPP), a measurement that equalizes the buying power of currencies—what *The Economist* has captured in their "Big Mac Index." The World Bank, rather than rely on GDP at market currency rates, uses such an adjusted figure to compare countries' standards of living. PPP establishes a set of comparable goods across countries and determines how many units of the local currency are needed to buy those goods in relation to a base currency (usually U.S. dollars). When GDP is adjusted by this recalculated exchange rate, the figure is effectively adjusted to mirror the real purchasing power. If a Big Mac costs $3 in New York but around $4 in London because of the exchange rate, it indicates that the British pound may be overvalued. Not a perfect methodology, but it but it begins to take more into account than simple dollar GDP.

In a globalizing world, it's useful to know how America's economy and currency are doing relative to those of other countries. For much of the 1970s and 1980s, many emerging markets were isolated economies and suffered from inflation and even hyperinflation (2,000% a year in Argentina). To stabilize their economies, many countries pegged their currencies to the U.S. dollar. These countries started trading and made gains. It largely worked, but in some cases it worked too well. When the U.S. dollar appreciated in the 1990s, financial crises ensued in Mexico, Asia, and Russia, among other developing places. Many were forced to abandon their pegs and freely float their currencies. This made them more competitive and, in tandem with help from the ITA, eventually transformed many into massive export machines, which added to America's trade deficit. Now most countries allow their currencies to float in value.

That's why if we don't use PPP or something like it, we risk creating a distorted picture of how we're really doing relative to other countries. If a country's currency devalues heavily, as Argentina's did in 2001, its economy looks dramatically different than it did just one year earlier. Argentina's shrank by two-thirds in dollar terms from 2000 to the end of 2001. Does that mean that Argentina produced and consumed only one-third as much in 2001? Not at all. There was a good chance that the amount of food consumed and goods bought were about 80-85% of what they were in 2000. But in U.S. dollar terms, the ultimate value looked much lower. PPP, therefore, helps remove some of the foreign exchange movements from the picture.

Let's examine a more recent situation. In 2012, Switzerland's aggregate GDP per capita in U.S. dollar market prices was $622 billion for a population of about 8 million - roughly $78,000 per capita. China's GDP in USD was $8.25 trillion for a population of 1.343 billion, or about $6,150 per capita. So a Swiss person, on paper, looked 12 times richer than the average Chinese person. But two distortions exist. During the Eurozone Crisis, many investors sought safety in the Swiss franc and pushed the currency to an overvalued level on a PPP basis. Conversely, in China the government has kept the currency weak on a PPP basis to continue fueling its export-driven economy. Taking into account the fact that the goods and services people need to sustain their standard of living are substantially cheaper in China than they are in Switzerland, and adjusting the GDP figures to reflect this, the PPP-adjusted per capita GDP drops to $45,300 in Switzerland and rises to $9,100 in China. Thus, the Swiss look only four and a half times as rich.

PPP adjustments, while not perfect, generally narrow the gap between rich and poor countries in terms of GDP levels. In fact, most people don't realize that since 1980 emerging market countries like China—former poor nations known as "lesser developed countries"—saw their economies grow from a low of 20% of the world's economy to roughly 50% based on PPP, thanks to their growing role in globalization. If we don't adjust GDPs by PPP, do we really understand how economies are faring in the world?

Figure 2.

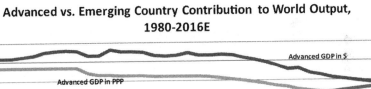

Advanced vs. Emerging Country Contribution to World Output, 1980-2016E

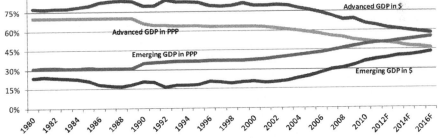

Source: World Bank

Inflation

Inflation, another economic indicator linked to GDP, helps adjust prices to suggest whether true purchasing power, therefore wealth, is rising or falling. Calculating a Consumer Price Index (CPI) helps us deflate nominal GDP increases caused by rising prices. This raises our first question regarding inflation: if it's not correctly calculated, then aren't *real* rates of GDP growth miscalculated, too? If CPI is rising, GDP is lowered by that amount. So there is an incentive to keep inflation low to help growth look better because so many elements of advanced economies hinge on GDP expansion or contraction, including interest rates, stock market multiples, and inflation-linked benefits, not to mention the fortunes of political parties.

Most countries price a basket of goods each month to track CPI. However, this basket is composed differently from country to country. In emerging markets, food can often comprise 50% of the basket, while in most wealthy countries it represents less than 15%. This means inflation rates in one country really can't be compared to another's without some serious analysis. In the U.S., the now-famous 1996 Boskin Commission report was organized on the premise that CPI was overstating inflation as calculated by the Bureau of Labor Statistics, which in turn was increasing liabilities in Social Security and other federal government retirement and compensation programs through "cost of livings adjustments" (sometimes referred to as "COLA").

Boskin explored two key ideas in his report: the "substitution bias" and "quality changes," what are called "hedonic" adjustments to the CPI due to substitutions and improvements that go into certain goods. To illustrate the substitution bias, Boskin noted that, when steak prices rise, people buy more hamburger and less steak, a substitution that results in less inflationary food prices. To demonstrate quality changes, meanwhile, Boskin showed how consumers get more for the same amount of money with each passing year. For example, a 27-inch flat screen TV might cost $500 one year, but a 30-inch model introduced the following year will go for the same price, which means hedonically the price of TVs is declining by more than 10%.

On the surface, these two ideas have merit, but let's take a deeper look. If people are substituting hamburger when steak prices increase, isn't that because prices *are* rising? By making this hamburger substitution, aren't we admitting that inflation is up? And to use the TV example, just because I'm getting more TV for the money doesn't necessarily mean I'm spending less for a TV. Yet, according to the Boskin methodology, this would register as *deflation*. So sometimes quality goes down, and we don't register it in inflation, sometimes up and we do. It's somewhat inconsistent and subjective, and since the report, statisticians have been making such quality adjustments on complicated goods and services like housing and healthcare.

The Boskin Commission accomplished what it was designed to do: reduce official inflation to reduce future government liabilities. The UK experienced a similar recalibration in the last decade with a switch from RPI (Retail Price Index) to CPI, also in an effort to reduce inflation-linked entitlements. This topic is continuously being debated, recently in the 2012 presidential election, which prompted the "chain weighted inflation" discussion, an arcane debate over mathematical calculations on CPI. And while the Boskin report and other recalibrations stem from honest attempts to refine the modern concept of inflation, to some extent, they may distort more than they clarify the picture.

All told, a decent dose of subjectivity goes into determining the official inflation rate. Considering the enormous impact small CPI changes can have across the world, it seems odd that there is so little transparency in these calculations. And what about regional inflations? Anyone living in the U.S. knows that many things, particularly housing, are more expensive in big cities like New York and San Francisco than they are in smaller cities like Nashville and St. Louis. And think about the regional differences in lifestyle: rising gasoline prices are far more important to someone who lives in a suburb and drives to work than they are to someone in Brooklyn who doesn't even own a car.

Let's consider the contents of America's CPI basket and the basket's proper weighting relative to real life in the United States. College education, housing, and health care costs have been rising faster than CPI rates for years. In fact, official inflation has risen overall by more than 105% since 1986, while average American college tuitions have risen nearly 500% in the same period. Since two years of college is now essentially a prerequisite to earning a median U.S. income, a case can be made for raising its slim 3.2% basket weighting, which was established decades ago. For a household making $50,000, 3.2% is only $1,600. Four years of tuition, room, and board at a good state college, on the other hand, probably costs $100,000 today. How can Americans say that education is only worth $1,600 of their basket if a family might have to put away multiples of that to save for college or other forms of advanced training over a lifetime? Of course, a more accurate weighting of college tuition in the CPI basket would probably result in a sharper increase in official inflation rates, triggering higher interest rates—not something desired by the government or Wall Street.

Inflation and Monetary Versus Fiscal Policies

The inflation debate is important not only in the context of consumer baskets but also as part of an even bigger philosophical obsession among government officials: interest rates and monetary policy. Ever since 1973 and the breakdown of America's fixed exchange rate policies, government officials have relied more heavily on monetary policy—as opposed to fiscal policies—as a thermostat to control the country's economic temperature. This has placed an enormous emphasis on the central bank to control inflation that, in turn, helps price interest rates and money supply.

Keeping inflation low is an important function. It stabilizes a country's currency value, lowers interest rates for borrowing (to keep GDP buoyant), and helps consumers maintain purchasing power and living standards. This was a big issue in the 1970s, when inflation seemed out of control, and is still a hawkish concern in places like Germany, whose people still remember hyperinflation between World Wars I and II, and in emerging markets like those of South America, where hyperinflation rates above 1,000% devastated Brazil and Argentina, among others.

But the obsession with inflation, like GDP, has led to another unintended outcome. By over-relying on headline inflation, central banks and elected officials have probably over-relied on monetary policy as the central lever over the U.S. economy—a practice emulated in many other countries. When GDP has slowed, central banks have lowered interest rates to get companies and people borrowing, creating a multiplier, or ripple effect through the economy. Lowering interest rates in America and elsewhere encourages people to buy houses or companies to borrow for expansion. As long as the activity doesn't create inflation, the policy seems sound.

But sometimes the lack of official inflation obscures problems, such as over-borrowing and asset bubbles. Economist Hyman Minsky noted that often prolonged periods of low interest rates create debt bubbles that are ugly when popped. In the housing market, mortgage securitization swelled by an extra $4 *trillion* from 2000 to 2007 as U.S. interest rates fell. In the corporate market, Minsky-minded economists focused on credit spreads—the premiums paid by companies above government rates—and saw them plummet during the boom. Indeed, over the last 30-plus years most economic crises have been largely financial busts. For much of American history, most economic slowdowns have been driven by business cycles of excess inventory (supply) mismatched with demand, with demand eventually picking up to take the country out of the recession. But recently, most crises seem to be driven by excessive liquidity (created by central banks) and subsequent asset bubbles. In other words, monetary policy may actually be the culprit.

Minsky would argue that the key barometer for monetary policy should be credit spread premiums,[3] because they are a better indicator for money demand and risk-taking. When spreads are super low and demand for money high, regardless of the actual inflation, Minsky would suggest that central banks should consider *raising* rates to curb future problems. Conversely, when spreads are high, indicating weak supply of credit, they should consider lowering rates. Interestingly, this could explain why now, some five years into the great slowdown,

---

[3] Credit spread premiums are the extra borrowing cost paid by companies above comparable US government interest rates.

short-term interest rates are near zero but the U.S. has failed to experience a material pick-up in borrowing to expand the GDP. That's because, as Minsky would argue, households took on too much debt before the crisis and are currently in the process of deleveraging and saving more. In times such as these, we might lean more heavily on classic Keynesian fiscal stimulus than on monetary policy, a strategy that Paul Krugman and other economists have called for since 2009.

But Americans set themselves up for this kind of crisis by relying on monetary policy instead of fiscal policy to guide the economy. It is far easier for elected and appointed officials to rely on interest rates and other monetary policies to boost GDP quickly than it is for those same officials to craft long-term social policies to create better human capital and a more sustainable, balanced economy. Such long-range planning would require compromise, sacrifice, and time to set structural policies in motion to change a variety of labor and consumption patterns—something not really possible with two-year election cycles in Congress. Just think about the 2012-2013 political gridlock surrounding America's federal debt ceilings: it's all about fiscal policy. Monetary policy, in essence, has become the crack cocaine for managing our economy. We get a quick boost, but we're left addicted to debt and even lower interest rates.

Many would argue that the U.S. would have been better off pursuing fiscal policies that steered citizens away from personal consumption and toward saving, that built export competitiveness, and that relied less on imported energy. But that's hard work for elected officials, hard work that would require several political maneuvers to recalibrate the country's incentive structures. It's so much easier to simply lower interest rates, which can also lower currency values, in order to boost borrowing and economic activity. But as mentioned earlier, toward what end? To expand GDP with unnecessary activity? To keep people employed in precarious, dead-end work? To forgo higher education while billions around the world improve their productivity? No wonder America had an economic heart attack in 2008.

GDP Skew and Wealth Distribution

Finally, we've yet to examine wealth distribution—generally a taboo subject in the U.S.—and the skew of GDP growth.

Americans balance competing ideals: we want to believe ours is the land of opportunity, where every citizen has access to the same basic services, such as schooling and health care, in order to develop into productive members of society. At the same time, we reward hard work and ingenuity by allowing exceptional performers to keep the full fruits of their labor. In reality, tax and economic incentive structures over the last several decades have favored the latter over the former, creating inequality not seen in a century.

If we look at the chart below, notice the widening gap between average GDP growth per capita and median individual income. This happens when high income becomes concentrated in a few hands, pushing averages up but not medians. The incomes of the top 1% of earners have skyrocketed, and their share of total disposable income has more than doubled between 1979 and 2007 to reach nearly 20%. Moreover, among the top 1% of earners, the top 1/100th has experienced outsized income growth vis-à-vis the rest of the 1%.

Figure 3.

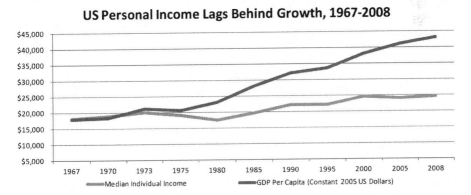

Source: US Census Bureau

31

Income and wealth dispersion can be better understood using the GINI coefficient. GINI is scaled from 0 to 1, with 0 representing perfect equality (where everyone has the same) and 1 representing a perfectly unequal society. In general, most countries around the world have better income distribution than the U.S., which, as we'll discuss a little later, has been steadily becoming less equal over the last two generations. Surprisingly, there are only a few countries with more unequal GINI coefficients than America (with and without social welfare transfers), and most of them are considerably less wealthy and not particularly stable. A high degree of income inequality implies a number of potentially undesirable consequences. Creating visible haves and have-nots can often lead to violence and revolution, but more often it leads to stress, envy, anxiety, political gridlock, poor health, and limited social mobility, which in turn can lead to a permanent underclass, putting democracy at risk.

The combination of envy and status-seeking amid growing inequality can be viewed as a root cause of the 2008 financial crisis, for it may have encouraged "subprime" borrowing by households intent on keeping up with the Joneses despite having less income than the Joneses. This economic polarization—and the desire to keep up—could also be what's driving the political splintering and gridlock and what's creating outrage movements as diverse as the Tea Party and Occupy Wall Street.

While many libertarians decry government monkeying with income distribution, denouncing it as "social engineering," empirical work by the nonpartisan Organization of Economic Cooperation and Development (OECD) has found little evidence that reducing inequality is harmful to GDP growth, even if GDP were our only goal. The OECD argues that by providing greater access to public services such as education and health care, and by thoughtfully reshaping tax policies, we can reduce inequality while increasing the "value of people." In terms of measurement and creating incentives, this means we need to subject GINI coefficients to as much scrutiny as GDP.

By now, we can see that GDP, while useful in many ways, is a substandard measure of the impact of public policies on improving the value of people. But GDP is not the only statistical fetish in global economics. Employment-related figures, too, are a point of obsessive attention that obfuscates the true condition of America's economy.

Employment and Unemployment

Most Americans would say that the government should create policies and maintain an environment conducive to people working and improving their lives. Government officials know this and try to capture certain statistics to determine how many people are working or not. Since the Johnson Administration, Washington has often linked GDP and jobs with Okun's Law. Named after Arthur Okun, LBJ's chairman of the Council of Economic Advisers, Okun's rule of thumb was that every 3% rise in GDP produced a 1% increase in employment (or a 1% decrease in unemployment). This purported correlation between jobs creation and GDP looked statistically sound for about a generation after World War II, and recent Fed Chairman Ben Bernanke had been known to use this rule of thumb. But with slow job creation during the most recent slowdown, the conventional wisdom of Okun's law has been statistically debunked, largely because globalization, demographics, and the Information Revolution have dramatically transformed the study and understanding of labor.

Even calculating unemployment, a seemingly easy counting exercise, has become far more art than science—and not a particularly good art. The way the Bureau of Labor Statistics (BLS) calculates these numbers, which relies heavily on self-reported data and landline phone surveys of several thousand people, is old school in the Information Age. Rather than create knowledge about labor, BLS employment numbers—and the underlying methodologies used to calculate them—lead to more questions than they do answers.

The unemployment rate is supposed to tell us how many people are employed in the workforce, but it says nothing about the *quality* or *security* of such jobs, which can vary dramatically with changes in economic cycles and consumer trends. The headline number used by policy-makers and laypeople alike is rarely qualified or explained. It is not easy to understand from this number alone whether true progress is being made.

Simple unemployment rates may have been informative in the past, but societies have changed dramatically since 1980, and even more so in the past decade. Automation and globalization have eliminated many American factory jobs and are even trimming others in places like China, which is losing out to even cheaper labor in countries like Bangladesh and Vietnam. But didn't the U.S. have unemployment rates below 5% for most of the 15 years prior to the crisis? What jobs were Americans doing that kept unemployment rates so low? Nobel Prize winner Michael Spence believes this American employment "success" was actually due to replacing millions of manufacturing and export-related jobs with low-wage, low-skilled work, such as joining a construction crew, doing interior decorating, or managing the paint department at Home Depot— domestic jobs that cannot be outsourced abroad. Unfortunately, these were marginal jobs. When the economy took a hit on both Wall Street and Main Street in 2008, these were the first to go.

Regardless of job quality issues, the question remains: how accurately are we calculating the true employment rate? Many argue that America's unemployment rate is much higher than the official figure. This confusion is rooted in an ever-changing definition of the eligible labor pool. In fact, the BLS actually computes *six different* versions of unemployment figures with varying definitions, with most people looking only at the most quoted headline number. The U.S. is not alone in these idiosyncrasies. While all OECD countries are supposed to use the International Labor Organization's definition of unemployment, most adopt their own versions.

Calculating the unemployment rate is seemingly straightforward: divide the number of unemployed workers by the total labor force. However, defining an unemployed worker (the numerator) and the total labor force (the denominator) is far from clear-cut. The U.S. headline unemployment rate is actually based on population surveys of people working, seeking work, or drawing unemployment benefits. Those who are still unemployed but who are no longer seeking work—i.e., the discouraged—statistically evaporate from the pool of eligible workers for headline unemployment.

For example, let's say there are 100 eligible workers and five can't find jobs. Most people would say unemployment is an easy calculation: 5%. One year later, the economy hits a rough patch and five more people lose jobs. Now we have 10% official unemployment. But let's assume that, of the original five unemployed people, three stop receiving benefits or looking for jobs—in official discourse, they become "discouraged." The way government statisticians adjust for this is to reduce the total labor force by three to 97. Official stats now show an eligible labor force of 97, with seven more unemployed, dropping the headline unemployment rate to 7.2%.

According to government statistics, if the same number of Americans were job-hunting today as in 2007, the official unemployment rate would be greater than 10%, not the last official rate of less than 7% in late-2013. The labor pool has been reduced by the so-called discouraged workers, who have permanently dropped out of the official numbers. Logic would tell us that more discouraged workers are a bad sign for any economy. Yet eliminating them from the labor pool, a practice first utilized nearly two decades ago, actually makes the official unemployment rate look better.

Below are the six ways the BLS calculates unemployment. As we'll discuss, each paints a different American labor picture:

U1: Rarely referenced, this is the percentage of workers (excluding active military personnel) who have been unemployed for 15 weeks or longer.

U2: Also used infrequently, this is the percentage of "job losers" (workers who have been involuntarily fired or laid off from their jobs) and people who have finished temporary jobs—generally larger than U1 but substantially less than U3.

U3: This is the official headline unemployment rate, the one touted by the media and politicians. This is the percentage of the civilian labor force that is unemployed but "actively seeking employment." It doesn't include people *not seeking* work, the so-called "discouraged workers." This U3 methodology was changed during the Clinton Administration to take in to account the people who had just stopped looking for a job. By creating this "discouraged" category, headline unemployment can be deflated as described above.

U4: This is the official BLS rate that is adjusted for the discouraged workers—i.e., this figure treats discouraged workers like other workers who are officially classified as unemployed. This makes the rate go up.

U5: This adds to U4 by including "marginally attached" workers in the unemployment rate calculation. Marginally attached workers are potential workers who have abandoned seeking employment for various reasons—maybe because workers are tired of looking, which places them in the discouraged worker category.

U6: This is the biggie. U6 adds to U5 by including part-time workers in the U5 unemployment rate calculation. The addition of part-time workers adds a few percentage points to the official unemployment rate.

The U6 rate is perhaps the most comprehensive measure of unemployment and underemployment available—and one that looks more like the way unemployment was calculated for much of the 20th century. As you can see below, when Lehman Brothers defaulted in September 2008, U3 was approximately 6%, but U6 was nearly double at 11%. U3 rose to approximately 10% in 2009 before dropping to below 8% in late 2012, about 2% higher than where it had been before the crisis began. However, U6 actually ballooned to nearly 17%—and only fell to about 15% by late 2012. U6 has actually deteriorated by 4% during the crisis, twice the rate of U3 deterioration.

Figure 4.

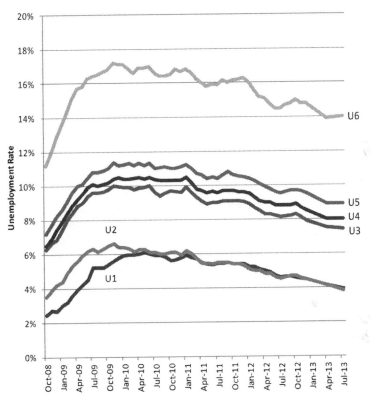

Source: Bureau of Labor Statistics

To compound the shortcomings of these six American unemployment calculations, our current figures also fail to consider the enormous disabled population in the U.S. About 57 million, or one in five Americans, live with disabilities. One in 10 has a severe disability. Some work, others don't. And every month, an eye-popping 14 million people receive a disability check from the government. Keep in mind that the U.S. only has around 140 to 150 million people in its official workforce. This 14 million dwarfs any monthly fluctuation of gains or losses in the headline unemployment rate, yet it receives little public attention. Federal disability payments to millions of Americans now tally more than food stamp and welfare programs combined. Yet because disabled Americans are not technically part of the labor force, they are not counted among the officially unemployed. Some hypothesize that the rise of disability is a reflection of limited job opportunities. It simply pays more and longer to be "disabled" than it does to be a "discouraged" worker who can't claim unemployment benefits anymore. Interestingly, in 1961 25.7% of American disability was due to heart disease or stroke, while only 17.9% was related to back pain, musculoskeletal problems, or mental/developmental issues, according to the Social Security Administration. By 2011, heart disease dropped to only 10.6%, while fuzzier, often subjective ailments like back/musculoskeletal/mental problems grew to 52%— and 52% of a much larger pool.

The U.S. unemployment picture is also distorted by America's swelling prison population, now some 2.5 million people and almost 2% of the official labor pool. That figure has increased fivefold since 1980, while the general population has only increased by 30%. In the *Freakonomics* world of economic statistics, prisons have added to America's GDP. Incarceration is big business. Sadly, America is now home to the most prisons in the world—some 4,575, or four times second-place Russia's 1,029. According to the Pew Center, America spent $52 billion to construct and operate those prisons in 2011, more than quadrupling the $12 billion spent in 1987. Keep in mind this doesn't include the *billions* spent on normal police activity. Again, common sense would indicate that a high prison population should not paint a rosier employment picture. As it happens, the magnitude of this distortion is unique to the United States, which has a prisoner-to-population ratio nearly eight times that of France or Germany.

While tracking the quality and quantity of employment is certainly important, policymakers should increasingly pay attention to called the "employment-to-population ratio" and "dependency ratio" – two related statistics that take into account what percentage of the population is working versus the percentage that isn't. Within those that aren't working fall people in school, those unemployed (and disabled), and those who are retired. Why are these figures important? Because ultimately they shed a lot of light on an economy's potential strength – particularly related to labor supply and domestic demand. According to the BLS, this rate hit 63% in 2007 before the crisis but now is around 58% – partially falling from aging Americans, but largely from the unemployment and disability issues we've just discussed. Looking forward, x-raying these demographic numbers – trying to see which age groups are participating and which aren't – should be a priority for policymakers given their impact on government programs ranging from education to Medicare and Social Security, as we'll discuss a little later.

Productivity: Working Hard, or Hardly Working?

Just as multiple definitions of unemployment distort the employment picture, so too has the reliance on traditional government calculations of "productivity," created by statisticians who simply divide GDP by number of hours worked. Headline productivity has been growing for the last couple of decades, but there is mounting evidence that something is off here, too. Many critics suggest that the strategic shift to worldwide sourcing designed to take advantage of lower costs is improperly captured in official statistics. Indeed, government statistical measures are simply not equipped to deal with the density of global supply chains that characterize the 21st-century economy.

The Progressive Policy Institute's Michael Mandel, the equivalent of a Bill James-style sabermetrician in economics, has written extensively on Washington's poor data infrastructure. In a paper with Susan Houseman of McKinsey & Co., Mandel suggests that increased productivity figures don't equate a more efficient national workforce. Let's say Ford Motor Company sources one million car parts from an Ohio-based supplier at $10 per part, for a total of $10 million. In one situation, Ford re-engineers its production process and reduces the number of parts it needs by half, dropping its cost of goods by $5 million, but it can still sell cars for the same price. This $5 million is recorded as a productivity gain. Alternatively, if Ford simply sources the same old part for $5 from China, the cost of goods also drops to $5 million. In either case, Ford's productivity goes up (sales minus the cost of materials), as does its profitability (sales minus cost of labor and materials) and measured productivity (value added per worker). These two scenarios are virtually indistinguishable in our productivity statistics. But while neither scenario helps the employment picture, one shows a country getting better, and one doesn't. In a globalized economy, statisticians cannot reasonably track all these underlying data streams to give us an accurate view on labor productivity or competitiveness. Such challenges bedevil most advanced supply chain economies.

What's Happened to Jobs?

Something has clearly happened to work in America over the last two generations. Discouraged and disabled people, plus the growing prison population, represent deteriorating labor markets that are possibly unprecedented since the Great Depression—it's tough to get a clear picture. No, America doesn't have visible mass unemployment, complete with long lines outside soup kitchens. Instead, it has millions collecting government unemployment or disability checks, plus 2.5 million more living in prison. What has happened?

Links between education, employment, and income have been studied for some time, but these relationships have changed profoundly during the last 40 years. The data suggest that, in this globalized era, advanced education has been rewarded in the labor market even as lower-skilled work has migrated to dozens of developing countries as we discussed. Anthony Carnevale at Georgetown University notes that in 1980 the lifetime earnings premium gained with a college degree was 40%. Today it's around 75%. Why did degree premiums almost double? Because, since 1980, the cognitive skills developed from higher education have been better rewarded.

Michael Spence's 2011 American labor study confirmed this, contradicting conventional wisdom that globalization is *only* about creating unemployment at home and keeping wages low by shifting production to cheap labor markets abroad. Spence's study found that, on the whole, globalization has in fact created employment opportunities in high-skilled sectors (such as technology, engineering, consulting, and finance) that are now able to take advantage of growth in Asia and other emerging markets. But, as Carnevale's work shows, you need more than a high school diploma to participate. Spence points out that low-skilled American labor now compete with 2.5 billion emerging market workers who are healthier and better educated than they were in 1980 (what Fareed Zakaria has called "the rise of the rest"). Fortunately, high-skilled brainwork is still in demand and cannot be so easily off-shored, although that will likely change in the future.

In order to maintain median income since 1980, Americans have had to study more. According to June 2011 census data, U.S. median household annual income approaches $50,000 and requires, on average, two years of post-high school education. For households without a high school diploma, income drops by nearly half to $25,157, which is considered poverty level in America. Add a college degree and the median soars to $82,846. Moreover, official unemployment levels among college graduates have been just above 4%, or around half the national average. An American medical or law school degree is a pretty good ticket to the top 15% in household income, even the elusive top 1%. Indeed, nearly a quarter of America's top 1% is comprised of doctors and lawyers.

Unfortunately, only 35 to 40% of Americans complete four years of college (and even fewer *in* four years). Carnevale reckons America's labor pool needs roughly *20 million more* post-high-school-educated workers to compete globally. And many studies suggest that this education gap is a root cause of the growing income inequality in America. If this is the first generation of Americans destined to be worse off than their parents, it's probably because this is the first generation since the early 19th century that is not better educated than their parents. Indeed, nearly one-quarter of Americans still don't even complete high school - a colossal public policy failure amid growing global competition.

In the future, globalization will continue to place a premium on higher education as Americans compete with the growing number of college-educated workers around the world. In the 1970s the U.S. had some of the highest global college graduation rates, but not anymore. Today, the country with the highest percentage of college graduates for 24- to 50-year-olds is South Korea (58%). In the U.S., that number is roughly 40%. And while the quality of some emerging educational systems can be questioned, the quantity of college graduates entering the global workforce is breathtaking. In 1978 in China, only 50,000 studied in universities. Today China enrolls 25 million college students—the most in the world—while America enrolls roughly 18 million.

The handwriting has been on the wall for some time. Why didn't Americans read it? Why weren't more Americans aware of their eroding competiveness? Because, back in 1980, the 40% premium for a college education wasn't all that attractive in our Nesting Nation. Why go to college at 18 when you could get a decent factory or house-building job in Ohio and make $15 dollars an hour, plus benefits? Why pay thousands in tuition when you could go into your family's construction or lawn care business? Yes, this may have made sense in a pre-globalized economy, but those factory jobs are gone now, outsourced to countries with cheaper labor. Likewise, nesting jobs like residential construction are less secure and very volatile.

The slowdown in American higher education trends has proven to be a terrible bet in the global era. The chart below shows the unemployment gaps in the recent slowdown relative to education gaps:

Figure 5.

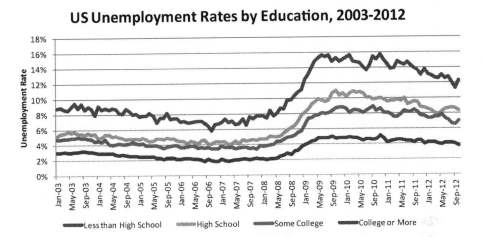

US Unemployment Rates by Education, 2003-2012

While there is a definite correlation between more education and more income, there is also evidence that the *quality* of American jobs, including the security of such work, has deteriorated, as well. These phenomena have truly confused our notions of "good" and "bad." Yes, any job is better than no job, but let's be fair: not all jobs are good.

Dean Baker at the Center for Economic Policy Research notes that, during globalization, America has been losing its ability to create sustainable jobs. Baker is another *Moneyball* economist who, looking beyond headline employment, devised more accurate stats to define what a "good" job means: it pays $37,000 a year (about $18.50 per hour) and includes employer-sponsored health care and an employer-sponsored retirement plan. Baker's statistics show that even though American workers are better educated than they were in 1979 (though not as highly educated as Carnevale would like to see), jobs that paid $18.50 an hour or more dropped from 82% of all jobs to 76% in 2010. If we then add the massive drops in health coverage and retirement plans, we see a stratum of what some call the "precariat," or precarious proletariat, whose livelihoods are tentative at best. In fact, we can see in the chart below that the U.S. didn't even have that many "good" jobs back in 1980—less than 30%—but that total dropped three to four percentage points by 2010.

Figure 6.

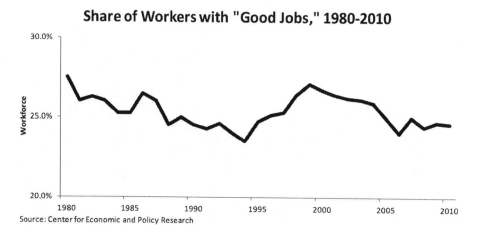

Share of Workers with "Good Jobs," 1980-2010

Source: Center for Economic and Policy Research

The precariat include many who opted to forgo college (and often high school diplomas) to work instead in housing and construction, undoubtedly fueled by the housing bubble that lasted from the late 1980s through 2007. To many it appeared an easy decision, but as the chart below shows, construction work has been incredibly volatile and closely mirrors America's boom-bust rollercoaster economy from 2000 to 2007. Note that construction unemployment rates dropped to roughly 5% in late 2006, only to jump to more than 25% in early 2010. During that same period, manufacturing jobs remained fairly stable. It's as if this unemployment spike in the U.S. was solely the result of the sudden slowdown in construction.

Figure 7.

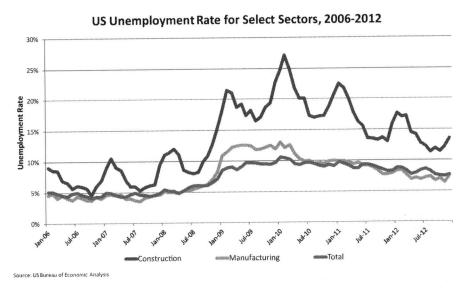

US Unemployment Rate for Select Sectors, 2006-2012

Source: US Bureau of Economic Analysis

But given residential construction's role in our nesting nation, this shouldn't surprise us. In fact, much of the annual new GDP growth from 1990 to 2006 was linked to residential construction, which almost doubled from 3.25% of GDP in 1990 to more than 6% in 2006. So we can see the double-effect of this phenomenon statistically: headline employment declined, while GDP rose—a win-win for politicians. The rosy numbers acted as a statistical smokescreen, obscuring the view of anyone not delving beyond headline employment and GDP.

If we factor in discouraged and disabled workers, prison inmates, and the proliferation of "bad" jobs, we must acknowledge that headline unemployment figures are misleading. Several million "good" jobs have been lost, replaced by a few million less "bad" jobs. Many millions simply don't work and have stopped looking for jobs. Official unemployment numbers looked good as millions took precarious, insecure jobs in construction—until construction stopped booming. At the same time, America's prison population is bursting with more than two million people, most of them minorities from economically deprived segments of society. This further underscores the poor state of American job creation. In failing to foster "quality" or "quantity" in the U.S. workforce, Americans have forgotten Englishman William Petty's lesson about the value of people.

For those lucky enough to attend college and maybe earn an advanced degree, things probably don't look so bad. Unemployment rates have been low—about half the official U3 rate. But even in that group, there's evidence that recent college grads in particular are "underemployed"—and not working in their fields of study. The Associated Press reported that about 1.5 million, or more than 53% of bachelor's degree-holders under the age of 25, were jobless or underemployed in 2011, which was the highest level since the Dot-com bust in 2000.

Figure 8.

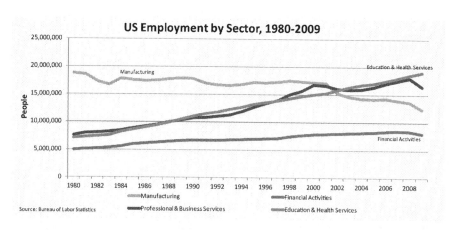

Most Americans today would be shocked to learn that, despite so much unemployment, the country is suffering labor shortages. A 2012 Manpower Group talent survey found that 49% of 1,200 key U.S. employers are experiencing difficulty filling mission-critical positions. In 2010 that figure was at 14%. The number of U.S. employers struggling to fill positions is at an all-time survey mark, despite high official and unofficial unemployment rates. This is telling us something unflattering about the U.S. workforce: public policies haven't properly planned for the skills that are in demand in this brave new economy. In short, America has been failing to improve the value of its people. And the U.S. can't simply push a button to overhaul its workforce; it takes time, although strategic immigration could help a bit in the short run.

Few anticipated the competition that arrived with globalization. In the last 30-plus years, *hundreds* of millions of people in dozens of countries have acquired skillsets that allow them to compete with American workers. So who's to blame for this? Who's responsible for keeping America's workforce competitive? Individuals or government? Both.

Individuals are responsible for their own actions, but government should have had the foresight to keep America competitive during globalization. Government can take an active role in developing human capital and improving productivity in everything from public education, health, and infrastructure to immigration. It can use tax policy to shape desired outcomes. But many in government have neglected those responsibilities, choosing instead to take comfort in the official headline employment figures instead of using a wider range of employment data to diagnose impending skills gaps.

What have these developments and policy failures done, in aggregate, to America? Looking at the last four to five decades of America's GINI coefficient shows a steady deterioration. This gets to the heart of our discussion of economic activity, education, unemployment, and equality. As globalization marches on, those with sufficient education to work as professionals for multinational corporations, tech companies, banks, and financial firms are enjoying the ride. So, too, are lawyers, consultants, engineers, and doctors. But large segments of America have simply been on the slow boat to downward mobility. Since the mid 1960s, the American GINI coefficient (with social transfers) has climbed from roughly the high .20s to the high .30s – a huge statistical change. Indeed, the relatively egalitarian America that I was born into seems to have steadily evaporated. Among 34 OECD countries, the US is now among the most unequal - surpassed only by much poorer countries such as Turkey, Mexico, and Chile.

The American Dream Becomes a Nightmare

If we study the economic history of the last half-century, recognizing the obsessive focus on GDP expansion and the effects of using misleading numbers for employment, trade, productivity, and inflation, America's postwar "boom" suddenly looks less impressive. Indeed, we can view the Great Recession/Reset/Slowdown as the inevitable byproduct of feathering our Nesting Nation, all while relying on misdirected government incentives and poor statistics.

The United States grew rapidly after World War II while Europe and Japan were reindustrializing. By all estimates, the U.S. had no real economic competition for as much as 35 years. Domestic energy was cheap and plentiful. Credit was relatively cheap and encouraged. Americans forgot about the wars and the Depression and bought and built houses in the suburbs. Domestic factories manufactured most of the objects that filled these new homes. New roads connected these suburbs, and the cars that filled them were largely made in Detroit. Women, most of whom were housewives before the war, began entering the workforce, and their labor was recorded in the formal economy. GDP rose. By the 1960s, when American lifestyles outstripped domestic production, Japanese and European imports arrived, bringing cheaper goods, cars, and foreign oil. Americans bought more, and official GDP hummed along for decades, punctuated by shallow recessions.

As America entered the postindustrial era, employment began shifting away from manufacturing toward the retail and service sectors. Old factory work gave way to jobs in the booming housing sector: contractor, interior decorator, mortgage banker, Wall Street financial engineer. America's focus turned increasingly inward at the very moment the world was globalizing. Home ownership grew steadily from less than 50% in 1945 to almost 70% by 2004 (it has since fallen to roughly 65%). We built condos. We built gated communities. We built townhouses. We spent trillions connecting these sprawling suburbs with vast highways and road systems, as well as regional airports, while neglecting to invest in the type of railroad transport systems found in Japan and continental Europe. These highways led to shopping malls and restaurants and gas stations. All this was supported by tax legislation that allowed mortgage interest deductions—a massive subsidy of the American Dream. The U.S. created Freddie Mac and Ginnie Mae to help guarantee mortgages, paving the way for securitized mortgages. The U.S. even created "subprime" mortgages to allow those who could not truly afford this extravagant nesting lifestyle a shot at the American Dream. House prices only went up over time—that was the conventional wisdom—so why not let everyone get their fair share?

The U.S. developed a localized system of public education, one that was largely—and perversely—based on property taxes. America's public schools were funded by the taxes people paid on their homes. "Good" neighborhoods and expensive zip codes boasted higher property taxes and thus better-funded schools, which meant higher college acceptance rates for the children lucky enough to live in affluent areas. This would prove to be a crucial aspect of income distribution in America, an issue at the heart of the Occupy Wall Street movement. Many Americans recognized this trend and stretched themselves financially to buy bigger houses in order to ensure their children's access to good schools. And why not? America's tax regime subsidized not only mortgage interest but also higher property taxes. Falling interest rates, fueled by an overreliance on monetary policy, helped, too. Americans nested more. We built bigger houses.

All the while globalization continued apace. More people from poorer countries around the world went to school. As their governments adopted free trade and market policies, these countries slowly entered the global economy. As they built factories, America imported more and more goods from them. And after the Asian financial crisis in the 1990s, many of these countries floated their currencies, driving down the cost of their goods but accelerating competitiveness on world markets. The U.S. trade deficit began to grow and grow. The once closed economies of Asia, Latin America, the former Soviet Union, and socialist regimes everywhere started to build and export goods to help Americans fill their ever-growing houses. Our trade deficit swelled. The U.S. built bigger and bigger cars and SUVs, even though family size had been decreasing steadily since the 1950s. These bigger cars required more imported energy, and the bigger houses needed more electricity and oil than ever before.

At the start of the new millennium, the American Dream gave way to a Nesting Nation bubble. The combination of the NASDAQ meltdown of 2000 and the horror of 9/11 led Americans to retreat further into their nests. The U.S. dropped interest rates, built more and more houses, took on bigger and bigger mortgages, securitized them and sold them to everyone around the world. The linkages to foreign countries deepened.

Emerging market economies, flush with trillions from exporting to America (along with England, Spain, and a few other spendthrift European countries), decided to hold onto their newfound wealth. What did they invest in? The most liquid bonds in the world: U.S. Treasuries. The recycling of these export earnings back into these bonds kept U.S. interest rates low. When rates seemed too low, what did these countries start to invest in? U.S. mortgage securities guaranteed by Freddie Mac and Ginnie Mae—that is, the U.S. government. And America's national debt grew.

GDP driven by consumption and government deficit—plus a steady decline in American interest rates and a belief that monetary policy could control the economy with the precisions of a thermostat—kept asset prices high and the American Dream seemingly within reach. At the same time, globalization and complex supply chains concealed shaky statistics regarding the quality of American life. Government and households borrowed and spent more, fueling GDP growth, but left America with huge debts. Similar traits surfaced in Western Europe, flowing outward to the continent's fringe as formerly communist countries in eastern and central European entered market-based economies. All of their economic doctors told Americans they were fine, to keep doing what they were doing, but in reality the heart attack was looming.

Bear Stearns was rumored to be in trouble because of overexposure to mortgages in early 2008. Six months later, cardiac arrest: Lehman Brothers went bankrupt. Banks all around the world no longer wanted to lend or trade with other banks, fearful that these counterparties would go bankrupt, too. Lehman held hundreds of billions in mortgage debt, and no one wanted to buy U.S. mortgage securities anymore. A month later, the U.S. Treasury had to broker deals to save the banking system. With car sales dropping 50% in late 2008, the government then propped up General Motors and Chrysler. Official unemployment hit 11.3%, but it was much higher if we looked deeper into the numbers—perhaps as high as 20% if "discouraged" and "disabled" workers were included, too.

The crash in late 2008 alerted America and the world to the vulnerabilities of America's inward-looking economy in an increasingly global world. Economists claim the U.S. is regaining its health, although near zero interest rates and quantitative easing, a new monetary policy maneuver designed to prop up the economy, are like morphine running through the country's system. Nevertheless, many in America and abroad are still feeling a lot of pain.

If economists and political scientists were to consider what progress really means in the modern world, then new ways of measuring, analyzing, and gathering data might more accurately reflect our holistic well-being. They'd all become sabermetricians, Big Data policymakers. We would no longer rely on old rules of thumb and conventional wisdom that aren't backed by convincing evidence.

With a clearer and more realistic understanding of the economy, better policies could be crafted to prevent future crises. By going beyond simple GDP and looking at a broad array of timely data, we can better diagnose our economic health. In the global age, new economic thinking needs to be aimed at developing human capital, which means building sustainable individual and public capacities, not blindly stoking GDP. By digging deeper into trade data and devising a truer statistical picture of labor, productivity, and employment, we can determine how human capital should be cultivated to remain competitive, returning our economy to a balanced, healthier state. Economists need look no further than to one of our greatest patron saints, Joseph Schumpeter, who described capitalism as an evolutionary process of continuous innovation and "creative destruction."

In the next sections, we'll discuss several concepts, alternative measures, and adjustments that can help us better define where we want our economy to go—and how it can take us there.

II
Brave New Math:
Redefining Objectives and Metrics

"Not everything that can be counted counts,
and not everything that counts can be counted."
—Albert Einstein

"Create all the happiness you are able to create:
remove all the misery you are able to remove."
—Jeremy Bentham

"A wealthy man is one who earns $100 more
than his wife's sister's husband."
—H.L. Mencken

"The biggest disease today is not leprosy or tuberculosis,
but rather the feeling of being unwanted,
uncared for, and deserted by everybody."
—Mother Theresa

There's a story commonly repeated on Wall Street, one popularized in Seth Klarman's book, *Margin of Safety*. It goes something like this: Sardines disappeared from their native waters off Monterey, California. With less supply, commodity traders bid them up, and prices soared. One guy bought a truckload of sardines at a nickel a tin. He resold them for a dime a tin to somebody else, who resold them for a quarter a tin to somebody else, who resold them for a dollar a tin to a fourth person. Shortly thereafter, the market for sardines collapsed and the fourth guy couldn't sell them, so he figured he might as well eat them. He opened the first tin, only to find the sardines rotten. The second and third were just as bad. So he went to the guy who sold him the sardines for a dollar a tin and said, "Those sardines you sold me were spoiled. Can I have my money back?" The seller looked at him and replied, "Oh, you don't understand. Those weren't eating sardines. Those were trading sardines."

Most of us would agree that, in the big picture, the purpose of commerce should be to create goods and services that improve the human condition—not simply to trade essentially worthless sardines. Economics shouldn't be about speculating blindly, creating a whirl of financial activity for its own sake, or bidding asset prices to ridiculous levels beyond value. We should not try to pump up our GDP to levels that have little connection to our own lives.

From its very inception, economics was a discipline meant to serve our well-being. The term "economy" derives from the Greek *oikonomia,* meaning "the management of the household." Aristotle considered economics intrinsically linked to moral and political philosophy and believed *oikonomia* to include only commercial activity that was meant to improve the quality of the lives of people, families, and households. By contrast, Aristotle also spoke of *chrematistike,* commercial activities that didn't necessarily enhance our lives. I think U2 said it more simply: "you can never get enough of what you don't really need." Clearly America has been focusing on "chremastics" for the last couple of generations, not economics in the classical sense.

Who hijacked the Aristotelian notion of economics and well-being? Oddly, the same architects that shaped our notions of what a country is all about: the empiricist thinkers of the Enlightenment. Throughout the 17th and 18th centuries, men like Thomas Hobbes, John Locke, David Hume, Adam Smith, and David Ricardo, among others, collectively helped forge philosophies and social principles on labor, economic incentives, trade, law, and taxation. Coupled with the scientific advances of those eras, these ideas helped propel the Industrial Revolution and raise human living standards. Indeed, up until this period, economic output grew very slowly—perhaps 0.1 to 0.2% per annum, according to the historian Angus Maddison. To put this into perspective, this means that output doubled every 500 years or so. At a global growth rate of 5%, formal output can double in less than 15 years.

While technology clearly has improved output, so has social organization. Americans sometimes forget that their forefathers came to the New World not only for religious freedoms but also for economic freedoms. In America, talent and hard work, not royal birthright, determined your future. Armed with the great Enlightenment theories of the time, America served as a bold experiment in meritocracy. Adam Smith explored many of these concepts and introduced the seminal idea that a market-oriented economy is a self-regulating system, whose rules are immutable scientific laws rooted in observed principles of human behavior.

However, this same empiricist shift in perspective may have also served to dehumanize the field. No longer was economics a means to serving a human end. As a self-governing market-based system, the economy was viewed as complete on its own. Smith suggested that individual actors motivated by self-interest would indirectly serve the greater social good, so there was no need to seek a greater purpose for economic activity. The market, guided by the "Invisible Hand," was the be all and end all. In this way, contemporary economics and the key tools we use to measure economic activity were designed to be impersonal and agnostic to human well-being. It became, in the words of Thomas Carlyle in 1839, the "dismal science," playing on the contrast to the phrase "gay science," which referred to "life-enhancing skills and knowledge," such as poetry and philosophy.

About a century after Carlyle came the Great Depression and what we might call the two great economic discoveries of the 20th century: GDP and mortgage Keynesianism. After World War II, it truly looked as if America had found some magic pixie dust. With GDP as our guidepost, we Americans achieved soaring, unrivaled output. Our children were the best fed, tallest, and the brightest. We built big, shiny cars and spacious homes, the best universities and best managed companies, the tallest buildings, and the longest bridges. We landed on the moon. It was, for most Americans, a golden interval. Indeed, during this period the bottom 99% of incomes in America actually grew faster than the top 1%.

But something interesting started to happen in the 1970s: America began to lose its mojo. GDP continued to rise, with only brief respites, but something happened to America's psyche and social fabric. Some conservatives say it began with loose morality in the 1960s and the breakdown of traditional families. Others cite political blunders like the Vietnam War, Watergate, and the Teheran hostage crisis. Some lament the loss of family farming and factory work—and the subsequent dissociation from manual labor. Some economists point to the end of Bretton Woods, the system of fixed exchange rates in place from 1944, and to the two oil shocks in the 1970s that ushered in globalization and a more competitive global economy. Many feel Americans simply lost their way.

Curiously, this psychic stagnation or lost sense of progress is not only an American phenomenon but one that can be observed in other advanced countries, such as the United Kingdom. Notably, GDP has continued to rise over the last 40 years in the U.S. and in other wealthy countries, but surveys of happiness haven't shown much improvement. Some have called this the "Esterlin Paradox," based on Richard Esterlin's 1974 paper, "Does Economic Growth Improve the Human Lot?" Esterlin found that, within a given country, people with higher incomes are more likely to report being happy. But once they get to a certain level, increases in income don't yield significant improvements in happiness. Indeed, once they scale the first two levels of Abraham Maslow's pyramid, meeting their physiological needs and securing their safety, they enter a new psychological realm, at which point they seek varying forms of happiness and well-being rather than pure GDP gains.

Figure 9.

Maslow's Pyramid of Human Needs

In fact, this happiness space—and how to measure it—is now a mushrooming multidisciplinary field that includes behavioral economics, neuroscience, psychology, philosophy, and sociology. Having garnered a huge amount of attention in the last decade, it speaks to Aristotle's notion of a good life. Particularly since the global slowdown, dozens of alternative metrics to GDP have been created. Clearly, some of these indices make more sense for some countries than for others, given each country's varying state of socioeconomic development and income. Some rely purely on quantifiable data, while others focus on more qualitative data. All of these indicators have pros and cons, and a 2011 report for French President Sarkozy, written by Nobel laureate Joe Stiglitz, Amartya Sen, and Jean-Paul Fitoussi, offers an excellent introduction to many alternatives and their underlying philosophies.

Alternatives to GDP

Some traditionalists and supporters of GDP believe that alternate measures or adjustments to the way we currently measure GDP are too subjective. However, current GDP is hardly value-free. As Cobb, Daly, and Halstead noted in 1995: "To leave social and environmental costs out of the economic reckoning does not avoid value judgments. On the contrary, it makes the enormous value judgment that such things as family breakdown and crime, the destruction of farmland and entire species, underemployment, and the loss of free time count for nothing in the economic balance. The fact is, the GDP already does put an arbitrary value on such factors—a big zero." As Robert F. Kennedy once declared:

Our gross national product—if we should judge America by that—counts air pollution and cigarette advertising and ambulances to clear our highways of carnage. It counts special locks for our doors and the jails for those who break them. It counts the destruction of our redwoods and the loss of our natural wonder in chaotic sprawl . . . Yet the gross national product does not allow for the health of our children, the quality of their education, or the joy of their play. It does not include the beauty of our poetry or the strength of our marriages, the intelligence of our public debate or the integrity of our public officials. It measures neither our wit nor our courage, neither our wisdom nor our learning, neither our compassion nor our devotion to our country; it measures everything, in short, except that which makes life worthwhile. And it tells us everything about America except why we are proud that we are Americans.

In 1972, American economists William Nordhaus and Nobel Prize winner James Tobin attempted to ascertain whether GDP growth was obsolete and came up with what they called the Measured Economic Welfare Indicator, which they found to be highly correlated with GDP from 1929 to 1965. About 20 years later, Cobb and Daly developed an offshoot of the Tobin-Nordhaus gauge called the Genuine Progress Indicator (GPI). GPI begins with the standard GDP statistic and adjusts for the previously hidden costs of climate change, crime, inequality, and resource depletion. It also incorporates borrowing and investing, time spent volunteering, and commuting into a holistic algorithm to parallel standard GDP.

<u>Redefining Progress's Genuine Progress Indicator</u>

+ Personal consumption weighted by income distribution index
+ Value of household work and parenting
+ Value of higher education
+ Value of volunteer work
+ Services of consumer durables
+ Services of highways and streets
- Cost of crime
- Loss of leisure time
- Cost of unemployment
- Cost of consumer durables
- Cost of commuting
- Cost of household pollution abatement
- Cost of automobile accidents
- Cost of water pollution
- Cost of air pollution
- Cost of noise pollution
- Loss of wetlands
- Loss of farmland
-/+Loss of forest area and damage from logging roads
- Depletion of nonrenewable energy resources
- Carbon dioxide emissions damage
- Cost of ozone depletion
+/- Net capital investment
+/- Net foreign borrowing
= GPI

Some of the big adjustments made by GPI include taking care of households, children, and the elderly; cleaning and making repairs; and contributing time to nonprofit groups. All of these are totally ignored in the GDP because money doesn't change hands. GPI adds back the value of this work, using the approximate market cost to pay someone else to do it. Crime is bad for an economy, but it adds to GDP by demanding billions to deter it and fix the damage it causes. GPI also looks at environmental degradation and harm by reducing "regrettables" in society—money spent on repairs after natural disasters or on defense against environmental degradation (air and water filters, for example). As we use up oil, wetlands, and other resources, this should appear as a negative cost on the national accounts, an amortized depreciation, just as it does for private companies.

Studies have shown that free time is something that people often value more than money. GPI calculates how much free time is lost and puts a value on it—an average wage rate. This reflects the opportunity cost of longer hours at work, including time made unavailable for family, travel, hobbies, and education, the latter of which could actually help improve income in the future. And finally, GPI adjusts GDP for improving or deteriorating wealth equality in society.

Figure 10.

To include such factors is to begin to paint a picture of the economy that more closely resembles what most Americans experience, rather than what GDP captures. GPI since 1950 shows the U.S. growing progressively through the early 1970s and then flattening. GPI suggests that the true costs of GDP expansion have begun to outweigh the benefits, resulting in growth that is actually uneconomic. In some areas, Americans may actually be backsliding. Specifically, GPI reveals that much of what we now call economic "growth," "progress," or "expansion" is probably just one of three blurred activities: spending to fix past mistakes (addressing "regrettables" means spending *trillions* in medical costs to remediate overconsumption), depleting resources that will be unavailable in the future, or shifting functions from unofficial work in the household and community to the realm of the official, monetized economy. Yes, GDP has essentially gone up and up and up since World War II, with few exceptions. But when we take into account many of the adjustments suggested by GPI, we begin to think differently about economic and social health. Moreover, given what we've already discussed about per capita and PPP distortions, it seems absurd that governments around the world, regardless of their varying levels of socioeconomic development, have anchored virtually all economic policies to expanding GDP.

One of the first U.S. states to use a customized version of GPI is Maryland, whose economy, like the federal one, has shown similar gaps between GDP and GPI beginning around 1970. The Maryland GPI also adjusts for how many people in the state have completed or are studying for college degrees, as well as for the number of people affected by divorce or underemployed. One of the most comprehensive studies of GPI versus GDP was released in 2013 by lead researchers at Australia National University who analyzed trends from 1950-2003 for 17 nations' economies. Their findings confirmed the Esterlin Paradox: many social and environmental problems have cancelled out GDP's rise over the last 30 years.[4] Moreover, the study not only found this to be true in advanced economies, but also in poorer developing countries such as China and India where gross GDP gains were negated by rising inequality, environmental degradation, and loss of leisure time, among others.

---

[4] Oddly, Japan was the only country to rise steadily through 2003 – even after years of sluggish GDP growth. The researchers believe that Japan's flat GINI and relatively light environmental footprint may have shaped this trend.

Figure 11.

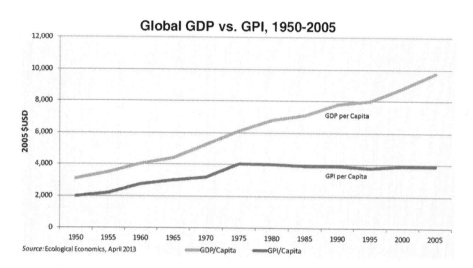

GPI has its own set of problems, since a lot of its numbers—like volunteerism and housework—are tough to calculate accurately. But it begins to integrate new sensors of well-being, forcing us to ask more questions about what our economy should be about, and begs for wider and more accurate data collection. Consider food labels. There was once a time when ingredients weren't even required for food packaging. But in 1965 the USDA required them, and Americans suddenly realized that there were chemicals and preservatives put in basic food, stuff most people couldn't even pronounce. Since 1990, calorie count and nutritional breakdowns have been added to food labels. Whether people want to keep eating chemicals and empty calories is another issue, but the availability of that information is now publicly mandated and has begun to seep into buying and eating behaviors. That's what new information sensors do: they broaden and deepen the knowledge base, expand public debate, and hopefully nudge people toward better outcomes.

Dozens of alternative measures exist. Many are offshoots of GPI, with several focusing on "green" or environmental data related to everything from carbon emissions and deforestation to global fish catches. The OECD has developed a "Better Life Index," a composite of 11 broad topics that include housing, income, and jobs, as well as quality of life (community, education, environment, governance, health, life satisfaction, safety, and work-life balance). The index, which allows each user to customize weightings according to his or her individual notion of a "better life," already includes the 34 OECD member countries, and plans are afoot to expand to partner countries, including China, India, Indonesia, Russia, and South Africa.

Some indices focus on "softer" data regarding well-being and attitudes. Ron Inglehart, a pioneering social scientist at the University of Michigan, has been producing his World Values Survey for almost 30 years. The survey covers more than 40 countries and poses dozens of questions to help construct an index of subjective well-being that reflects happiness and general life satisfaction. In 2005, the tiny Himalayan nation of Bhutan developed the Gross National Happiness Index, which takes into account health, culture, education, ecology, good governance, community vitality, and living standards in an effort to broadly assess progress beyond pure GDP growth.

One of the more interesting yardsticks to be developed in recent years is the Legatum Prosperity Index, which mixes eight equally weighted sub-indices with 89 different variables for 142 countries. Two Legatum sub-indices are Personal Freedom (freedom of speech and religion, plus national tolerance for immigrants and ethnic and racial minorities) and Social Capital (including the percentage of citizens who volunteer, give to charity, help strangers, and are able to rely on family and friends). Similarly, Xavier University's American Dream Composite Index measures the extent to which people living in the United States achieve the "American Dream," defined by five sub-indexes and 35 dimensions from monthly surveys on everything from satisfaction with jobs and mobility to questions on diversity, safety, and trust in government.

One of the more comparative barometers for a country's economy amid globalization is the World Economic Forum's annual Global Competitiveness Index (GCI) that ranks more than 140 countries based on mix of empirical and subjective data. GCI is comprised of twelve "pillars" of competitiveness aggregating approximately 110 variables. Roughly two thirds of the GCI come from more than 13,500 Executive

Opinion Surveys, and one third comes from publicly available data. The current index, developed by Xavier Sala-i-Martin and Elsa Artadi, has also incorporated elements of Jeffrey Sachs's Growth Development Index and the Michael Porter's Business Competitiveness Index. Rolled together, GCI helps look beyond GDP and helps x-ray a country's infrastructure, government financial stability, educational attainment, and capacity for innovation, among many other "pillars" of economic competitiveness in our global world.

Like GPI, these relatively new indices force us to look at a wider range of well-being variables. Unfortunately, many rely heavily on subjective polls and surveys, which means that rankings and national mood swings can change quickly in ways most hardcore bio-social data do not. In 2012, for example, the U.S. fell from a top 10 Legatum country to 12th, partially because of a survey question about "confidence in financial institutions." Only 48% of Americans expressed such confidence, compared to the 61% global average. A year of bad headlines about JP Morgan and Goldman Sachs could easily sway such polls, but the notion that America's financial institutions are in worse shape than most globally is a bit farfetched. "Confidence" is a subjective term and will vary from country to country (and perhaps month to month). Perceptions, as we've discussed repeatedly, should not be confused with data.

One of the older data-driven benchmarks that explores real life issues for most Americans is the Institute for Social Innovation's Index of Social Health (ISH), composed of 16 indicators in the chart below. The premise of the ISH, adopted in 1987, is simple: "American life is revealed not by any single social issue, but by the combined effect of many issues acting on each other. In looking at social problems that affect Americans at each stage of life—childhood, youth, adulthood, and the elderly—as well as problems that affect all ages, the Index seeks to provide a comprehensive view of the social health of the nation." The ISH is appealing in that it also studies datasets of social ills across different age groups.

Figure 12.

Index of US Social Health

Children	Adults	All Ages
Infant mortality Child abuse Child poverty	Unemployment Weekly wages Health insurance coverage	Homicides Alcohol-related traffic fatalities
Youth	**Elderly**	Food insecurity Affordable housing Income inequality
Teenage suicide Teenage drug abuse High school dropouts	Poverty, ages 65 and over Out-of-pocket health costs, ages 65 and over	

ISH has fallen since 1970, similar to GPI, oddly paralleling America's psychological decline that has occurred alongside GDP's continued rise. While the U.S. has made some progress in infant mortality and high school completion rates, as well as homicide and alcohol-linked traffic deaths, ISH has been undercut by worsening trends in child poverty and child abuse, teen suicide, unemployment, weekly wages, and health insurance coverage, the last three echoing some of what Dean Baker observed about "good jobs" and America's precarious workforce trends. As the chart below notes, social health in the U.S. bottomed out in the early 1980s, bounced around in the 1990s, and rose again by 2000 without quite reaching 1973's high. Today Americans stand where they were in the late 1980s—much closer to the bottom than to the top.

Figure 13.

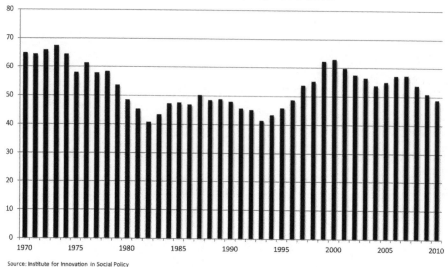

Index of US Social Health, 1970-2010

Source: Institute for Innovation in Social Policy

During the 1980s, frustration was also rising in lesser-developed countries. World Bank and United Nation experts were worried that GDP growth was not always translating into healthier children, greater education, and more gender participation in society. The pioneering work of Mahbub ul Haq and later Amartya Sen found expression in 1990 in the monumental UN Human Development Index (HDI), a dataset gathered annually that has been expanded and now includes health, education, inequality, poverty, gender, environmental sustainability, as well as innovation and other standard economic data like income. HDI changed the popular mindset regarding national well-being and forced many governments to look at a broader range of measurements outside of GDP, many of which went well beyond traditional economic measurements.

Sen's stated philosophy behind HDI sounded almost Aristotelian: "Human development is the process of enlarging people's opportunities and improving their well-being by building *capabilities*. Human development is dedicated not to how big an economy can swell, but to what ordinary people can do and what they can become . . . Because different people value different things, no comprehensive, universal list of capabilities applies to everyone. In the human development framework, a central concept is the freedom to decide for oneself how to live; a good life is a life of genuine choice." Choice is the key word. But as we'll see, choice is not merely freedom to choose. Sometimes we simply don't have the capacity to choose correctly.

Two former members of the HDI team, Sara Burd-Sharps and Kristen Lewis, have taken this approach one step further in their *Measure of America* project at the Social Science Research Council (SSRC). They promote a view that, along with measuring and fostering human development, asks the central question: "How are people doing?" The traditional question, of course, has always been: "How's our economy (meaning GDP) doing?" The SSRC has created an American Human Development Index (AHDI), a simplified version of the UN HDI, with the goal of monitoring three key areas of health, education, and income. By expressing a broader set of social data, these numbers explain in detail the seemingly intractable political gridlock and partisanship that has gripped America in recent years.

ADHI is comprised of four simple statistics in three sub-indices: life expectancy (the health sub-index), educational attainment and school enrollment (education), and median income (income). The SSRC then disaggregates these three by state and 435 congressional districts, as well as by gender, race, and ethnicity. A close look at this information reveals startling differences within the country—and begins to explain many of the frustrations felt today. In fact, as we compare congressional districts, we realize that America is really a land of many countries, with huge variations in human development often in close proximity.

For example, in the Los Angeles metro area, Orange County registered AHDI of 8.88 (on a scale of 1 to 10, with 10 being best) for the year 2012, while the Watts section of LA only totaled 1.91. Disaggregating the data tells an even more disturbing story: life expectancy in Watts is only 72.8 years, five years below the national average but a startling 14.4 years *lower* than Orange County's 87.2 years. In fact, life expectancy in Orange Country would be the highest in the world if the county was a *country*, ahead of world leader Japan by a remarkable five-plus years. If Watts were a separate country, on the other hand, it would drop to around 95th in the world (out of 198 countries), clustered in a group of largely developing nations like Egypt, Dominican Republic, Colombia, and Mauritius.

Education and income show similar gaps. In education, 53.8% of Watts's residents fail to complete high school, versus less than 4% in Orange Country. In terms of higher education, 55.3% have at least a bachelor's degree in Orange County, versus 3.7% in Watts. When it comes to them, only 1.1% of Watts' residents obtain advanced degrees, versus 21.2% in Orange County. As we would expect, these differences manifest themselves in median earnings: $51,632 in Orange Country versus $18,785 in Watts.

These disparities within the United States—and often within the same city—are breathtaking. For example, the wealthiest American congressional district, NY-14 on the Upper East Side of Manhattan, boasts median earnings of roughly $60,000. Just a few miles away, in District NY-16 (the Bronx), median earnings are roughly $18,000. State-to-state variations, too, are often large: Arkansas' median income is less than $23,500, while in Washington, D.C., it is $40,342 (no wonder Americans feel Washington is out of touch!). Washington also has among the highest rates of educational attainment, underscoring the growing relationship between learning and earning.

So how is America faring on this American Human Development Index? The answer really depends on how educated you are. If you went to college or grad school, you are probably living a healthier life, residing in a nicer neighborhood, and enjoying an above-average income. In turn, higher incomes reinforce better education, improving health ad infinitum in a virtuous circle.

If you're not that educated, you're probably making a below-average income, living in a bad part of town, with your kids attending a poor school. There's also a high statistical chance you'll live a shorter, less healthy life. This capabilities analysis is possibly the greatest indictment against America's GDP obsession, which has led to misguided data, poor inference, and bad government policy decisions. By focusing on simple headline GDP and U3 unemployment, the U.S. has created a lopsided society. Affluent areas of opportunity sit side-by-side with empty pockets of despair. Yes, Americans all have the same freedoms, but clearly they don't all have the same access to capacity-building and, therefore, the same opportunities.

Confusing Freedom with Equality of Opportunity

A country can only do well if its people are doing well, and virtually all Americans—Republicans and Democrats alike—believe every citizen has a right to enjoy a life of good health and a decent living standard. But, as the data suggests, only people with extensive, well-developed capabilities have the tools they need to realize this Aristotelian good life. Those lacking capabilities are less able to control their own trajectory and to seize opportunities. Without basic capabilities, particularly during globalization, human potential remains unfulfilled. However, herein lies the rub.

The American culture of rugged individualism is rooted in the notion that, if the government gives everyone freedom, everyone has the power to develop his or her capabilities—i.e., everyone has a shot at becoming the hero in a classic Horatio Alger story. Not so. In some ways, America has confused freedoms with capabilities and opportunities. Take education. All U.S. citizens have the basic freedom to go to college and earn a degree, and, as discussed above, this provides a pathway to better wages and a higher standard of living. Yet data suggests not all citizens have the capabilities to get into college or to complete a degree. Low-income students are significantly handicapped by poor health and low-quality public schools, not to mention financial constraints.

The reality is that being born into certain American locales condemns some citizens to a life of substandard health, poor education attainment, and low income, all of which are all bound together. As the SSRC emphasizes, "Formal freedoms are necessary but not sufficient to *provide true capabilities* to function. The capability approach to well-being, which prioritizes *the ability to actualize opportunity* into 'beings and doings' contrasts with other theories of well-being which focus on subjective measures, such as happiness."

So how can Americans improve their economy on all measurements, beyond GDP? As Amartya Sen and the SSRC preach: by simply improving people's capacities. Like losing weight, which requires diet, exercise, and, above all, discipline, this is often easier said than done. As we'll discuss later, there are several short- and long-term policies that can help build essential human capacities. But first Americans need to make human capacity a primary public objective, capture this data better and far more frequently than they do, and then craft policies toward improving such figures. While Americans are accustomed to following leading indicators like GDP, inflation, housing stats, and other financial data monthly or quarterly, they measure low birth weights, educational attainment rates, the number of children living in extreme poverty, and many other bio-social indicators only once every two to three years. The U.S. census, meanwhile, is taken only once every 10 years—an eternity in the Information Age.

Bad Economic and Social Policies = Inequality

Equality is one of the founding principles of American society. French historian Alexis de Tocqueville noted, "Americans are so enamored of equality that they would rather be equal in slavery than unequal in freedom." While the principle may remain dear, in reality, inequality has grown sharply over the last four decades. As the SSRC data notes, the inequality is not just in income but also in health and education.

On the income front, the income of those in the top 1% of earners has skyrocketed, and their share of total disposable income has more than doubled between 1979 and 2007 to reach nearly 20%. Occupy Wall Street lambasted the 1%, some three million people. Yet data suggest it is really the top 1/10th percent—approximately 300,000 people in a country of more than 300 million—that has seen a disproportionate share of income growth. The inequality goes even higher with the top 1/100th percent—only 30,000—enjoying an even greater disproportionate gain. Yes, in America's top 1%, there's an enormous gap between millionaires and billionaires.

Forbes magazine noted in March 2013 that America is home to 442 billionaires, about 1.43 per million people. There are now approximately 5.1 million millionaires in the U.S., or 1 in 60. Keep in mind that, since the global economic slowdown of 2008, 120 million Americans have watched their individual net worth shrink to $2,200. Millions more now have a negative net worth. Herein lie the seeds of America's discontent. Politicians just might be out of touch with average Americans. The U.S. Congress has 44 times as many millionaires as the general U.S. population in terms of percentages. Approximately two-thirds, in fact, are millionaires.

This extreme inequality means that, while all Americans have the *formal* freedom to pursue their goals, many lack the *effective* freedom necessary to achieve them. It's important to understand that, although it's rare to see in the U.S. the kind of absolute poverty found in developing countries - what it means to be poor or rich differs radically through time and from place to place. Before World War II, electrical appliances were rare in most American homes, while today appliances are nearly universal. However, that does not mean that everyone who has a refrigerator and a TV is necessarily rich.

Even Adam Smith, the father of modern economics, recognized that what is "necessary" is socially defined. Smith observed that it's not sufficient to have what we need to survive; we also need to have what is required such that we can walk in public without shame. As he wrote famously of the linen shirt in *Wealth of Nations*:

> *A linen shirt, for example, is, strictly speaking, not a necessary of life. The Greeks and Romans lived, I suppose, very comfortably, though they had no linen. But in the present times, through the greater part of Europe, a creditable day-labourer would be ashamed to appear in public without a linen shirt, the want of which would be supposed to denote that disgraceful degree of poverty, which, it is presumed, nobody can well fall into without extreme bad conduct.*

What is remarkable here is that, even in the 18th century, Smith realized that the linen shirt was more than just an article of clothing to keep people warm. The linen shirt shaped or signified something in other people's perceptions, which might change their behavior and increase their level of respect, thereby, improving the psychological well-being of the laborer. In the 21st century, such signal value is tied not only to items of clothing but to cars, houses, and educational credentials. Smith knew that well-being went beyond our relationship to material things; it also includes our relationships with other human beings. So when we think about GDP and economics, we need to focus not only on absolute well-being but also on relative well-being. In some ways, Smith was a proto-psychologist, or behavioral economist, in that he understood the power of inequality in society.

For many years, most governments and economists weren't too concerned if the rich were getting richer as long as absolute GDP was rising. The theory of "trickle down" economics held that wealth would work its way through the economic layers, eventually finding its way to even the poorest strata. Indeed, as has been discussed above, from the late 1940s to the mid-1970s, all American income groups were moving up the ranks while GDP expanded. But the reality is that *relative* wealth and income matter, too, because they reveal visible signs of success, such as the linen shirt. The buildup of wealth by a tiny percentage of Americans, combined with economic disparities, can create physiological and psychological consequences that affect not only people's current well-being but also their future well-being.

Income inequality produces a number of potentially undesirable consequences for all of society, not just for the poor. The toxic effects of inequality range from social to economic to political. In *The Spirit Level: Why More Equal Societies Almost Always Do Better*, Richard Wilkinson and Kate Pickett compare a number of advanced societies based on income inequality data and find that inequality generally correlates with shorter, unhealthier, and unhappier lives; increases the rate of teenage pregnancy, violence, obesity, imprisonment, and addiction; and drives excess consumption. It creates, essentially, an unstable economy.

History is littered with examples of deposed governments that lost their mandates when inequality became too great. We're not just talking about Marie Antoinette and pre-Castro Cuba. Contemporary, developed economies also suffer from political instability as a result of growing inequality. Alberto Alesina of Harvard University and Roberto Perotti of Bocconi University in Milan studied 71 countries and found that higher levels of income inequality were associated with increased social instability. They explain that unrest often erupts when a wealthy middle class is weakened. David Autor of MIT suggests that the U.S. middle class is currently suffering from these pressures, as a polarization of the labor force into high- and low-skilled segments comes at the expense of middle-skilled (and middle-wage) positions. Therefore, it's important for governments to analyze the distribution of gains in per capita income, prioritizing and reporting GINI as frequently as they monitor and report GDP.

Brave New Equality in Capacities and Opportunities

Not only should our brave new goals go beyond sheer topline and compositional GDP, which would mean more savings and investment and less consumption; they should also shape a better balance of prosperity. "Redistribution" tends to be a dirty word in many policy circles, but better income and wealth dispersion through thoughtful policies are necessary to ensure greater economic stability. Market forces are fine for supply and demand, but government often sets the tone for supply and demand based on a variety of policy incentives. Ask yourself this: how stable can demand be in an economy in which 10-20% of the population holds more than 80% of the wealth?

Interestingly, while they feel such inequality, most Americans don't have a clue just how unequal America has become. In a recent study, Dan Ariely of Duke and Mike Norton of Harvard found that Americans dramatically misunderstand economic distribution in the country and actually desire a substantially different income mix than what has evolved over the last 40 years.

Ariely and Norton asked more than 5,000 people the following question: "What percent of wealth do you think the bottom 40% and the top 20% of Americans possess?" The survey results were shockingly off: people answered 9% for the bottom and 59% for the top. But the reality is quite different: the top 20% holds a remarkable

84% of America's wealth, while the bottom 40% owns just 0.3%. In the years of economic growth between 2002 and 2007, 65% of the income *gains* went to the country's top 1% of taxpayers.[5]

Ariely and Norton then asked the same group to look at three different unnamed income distributions: one allocating 20% equally among five quintiles, one showing incomes similar to those in the U.S., and one resembling incomes in Sweden, which has some concentration of wealth at the top but not nearly as much as America has.

Figure 14.

Ariely/Norton Survey on Wealth Distribution Preferences

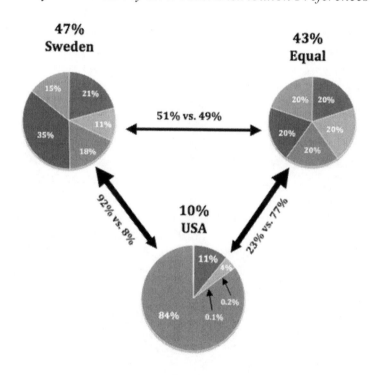

[5] This kind of data is also supported by the pioneering work of Thomas Picketty and Emmanuel Saez, who have looked at income distribution for the last 100-plus years. Nobel laureate Joseph Stiglitz and the World Bank's Branko Milanovic, among others, have also written extensively about it.

The Ariely/Norton study shows surprising gaps in perception, reality, and preferences in the data. True financial skew of income and net worth is vastly unequal and misunderstood. Of those surveyed, 92% preferred the Swedish over the American skew, and 77% preferred an equal distribution over the American distribution. And most were shocked that the top quintile in America held some 84% of the country's wealth (most thought it was around 59%).

Such surveys suggest Americans want a better distribution of income, but other data and studies point to different priorities. When it comes to money, as in many other aspects of life, emotions and feelings often trump human rationality. Countless surveys with questions such as this one—"Would you rather earn $60,000 a year while other people average $30,000, or would you rather earn $120,000 a year while other people average $200,000?"—show that more than half of us would rather make twice as much as other people, even if that means earning half of the other option. Irrational, but true. This result is one from among thousands of experiments in fields known as "behavioral economics," "neuroeconomics," and "evolutionary economics." Indeed, economists generally assume that humans act as rational actors economically, what is often called *homo economicus*. But this doesn't seem to be the case. Sadly, we are hardwired to care about the Joneses. In relatively high-income societies, relative social ranking tends to trump absolute income and wealth. Indeed, Glen Firebaugh of Penn State notes:

[What] matters most is not income per se but income relative to the income of one's peers. Americans compare themselves to other Americans of the same age, resulting in a hedonic treadmill because incomes in the United States rise over most of the adult lifespan. Rather than promoting overall happiness, continued income growth in rich countries could promote an ongoing consumption race where individuals consume more and more just to maintain a constant level of happiness.

If you're earning more than most of your friends, neighbors, and work colleagues, then guess what? You're probably happier than those in your social sphere who earn relatively less. That's what countless happiness surveys tell us.

This is also a key takeaway from the eye-opening 2012 research by the Federal Reserve Bank of San Francisco entitled, "Relative Status and Well-being: Evidence from U.S. Suicide Deaths." The study's authors hypothesized that suicide data provides an objective alternative measure of happiness (or unhappiness) with several advantages over previous studies that rely on subjective answers. It is assumed that those who've committed suicide are unhappy. After regressing suicide data and income down to county levels (an interesting Big Data experiment), the authors found that individuals committed suicide more frequently when income was lower relative to the income of others *in their local area*. In other words, there was a causal link between low relative incomes and suicides *within* counties. Again, people really do judge themselves against the Joneses.

And keeping up with Joneses—and the resulting economic "arms race" it has created over time—has been the focus of Cornell economist Robert Frank for decades. Much of Frank's work explores the power of what Fred Hirsch in 1976 called "positional goods," goods that help define social status because of their exclusivity. When we all try to one-up each other, we cancel out each other's efforts, which leads to spending for no good reason. We don't get the exclusivity that we seek, just as countries don't gain any additional security with more nuclear weapons. Frank argues that this has led to an American consumption arms race, which has left all buyers of positional goods—status items like fancy watches or cars or houses—worse off. In other words, when what we want depends upon what others have, a consumption "externality" arises, and our fruitless pursuits will be economically inefficient and wasteful.

In a 2010 working paper, Frank found that those U.S. counties in which income inequality grew the fastest also showed the biggest increases in symptoms of financial distress including divorce rates and lengthier commutes, among others. While the top few percent spend more because they have so much extra money, Frank notes:

[T]heir spending shifts the frame of reference that shapes the demands of those just below them, who travel in overlapping social circles. So this second group, too, spends more, which shifts the frame of reference for the group just below it, and so on, all the way down the income ladder. These cascades have made it substantially more expensive for middle-class families to achieve basic financial goals.

Seen in this light, income inequality probably contributed to the financial crisis by encouraging subprime borrowing and home-equity borrowing by households trying to make up for their lack of income.

In his *Darwinian Economy,* Frank lays out why such irrationality is futile and may have led to America's recent housing meltdown. Let's imagine the following choice: living in a 5,000-square-foot house while everybody else lives in a 6,000-square-foot house, or living in a 3,000-square-foot house while everybody else lives in a 2,500-square-foot house. Again, most people prefer the second world even though their house is 2,000 square feet smaller. Why? Well, because beyond a certain square footage of utilitarian space, housing is a positional good: we get additional satisfaction from a larger house, not only because it's bigger in *absolute* terms but also because it's better in *relative* terms to other families. That is, we get additional satisfaction from having more house than the Joneses. So we work harder to buy bigger houses.

But unfortunately, as Frank notes, the Joneses feel the same way—they're also working to buy a bigger house. So our relative satisfaction gain disappears because the bigger house is no longer better. This is the consumptive arms race in action. We are now merely keeping up with the Joneses, rather than trying to act rationally. In the U.S. the phenomenon has caused many Americans to buy more and more house than they (and the economy) really need, wasting money, creating unnecessary debt, and pulling more American labor into nesting jobs in the expanding housing sector.

This is why we need to rethink public policies. As noted earlier, we can never get enough of what we don't need. Solid public policy should protect us from such destructive impulses by nudging us in directions that don't hurt us physically or economically, as Richard Thayer and Cass Sunstein urge in their excellent book, *Nudge: Improving Decisions About Health, Wealth, and Happiness.* But in America, policymakers have actually instituted polices that promote reckless, inefficient spending to keep up with the Joneses, thus imperiling the country. How has this happened?

As we have discussed, home ownership and education policies are perversely bound together by property tax-based schooling. In America, school quality is determined by real estate values, with more expensive neighborhoods spending more on education than poorer ones. To send their children to a better school, Americans must outbid others for a house in a good school district with high property taxes. Yet when everyone keeps bidding for such houses, *all* housing prices are elevated.

Housing, per se, will probably always be some type of positional good, like fancy cars, jewelry, and clothes. However, a public educational system—one that is geared toward creating equal capacities and opportunities for all—should not link such school quality to real estate prices. In most American states, local public schools are monopoly suppliers funded by property taxes. With this incentive structure, the good schools get better while the bad get worse.

Often, the difference in school taxes and zoning—and resulting quality—can be quite profound. The telling American TV series *Friday Night Lights* showcased the pronounced difference between going to high school in the wealthier west side of Dillon versus the less prosperous east side of town. The *Measure of America* studies often cite grave educational differences within relatively close real estate markets. If we say it's a public policy imperative to build human capacities to remain competitive, we need to rethink a variety of policies that create equal opportunities, opportunities that don't broadly exist in today's America.

Beyond encouraging social and economic instability, inequality has public health implications and costs that we are only beginning to understand. The data underscore some interesting linkages: poor education often leads to poor health. And poor health costs America *trillions*—a huge tax on the economy. According to the nonpartisan Congressional Budget Office's *2011 Long-Term Budget Outlook,* at current trends Medicare and Medicaid costs are expected to balloon to approximately 11% of GDP by 2050. Unless the health of the country's poor is improved, health care costs will begin to tax the country in ways that imperil many needed government services.

Some of America's physiological woes are psychologically inflicted. Recent research bolsters Smith's linen shirt observation by showing that inequality can lead to poor self-esteem, lack of respect, and daily stress, which in turn can contribute to poor health. Many studies explore our genetic "fight-or-flight response" system. When we encounter perceived threats, including both mortal threats like a house fire and less acute threats like traffic or a stack of overdue bills, alarm systems in our brain and body are activated. What does this do? Studies at the Mayo Clinic and Johns Hopkins show that psychological stress creates physiological responses, including the release of cortisol and adrenaline, an increase in heart rate, and elevated blood pressure. Under normal circumstances, our bodies eventually return to a calm state, but if we're under constant stress, our systems never reset. As a result, the steady flow of cortisol undermines immune system responses and suppresses the digestive system, the reproductive system, and growth processes. It also alters the brain's ability to understand and control mood swings, as well as motivation and fear. If our systems never reset, a vicious circle ensues: the lack of control over potentially stress-inducing events creates more uncertainty, leading to even more stress, ad infinitum. Lengthy periods of being overstressed and overexposed to cortisol and other stress hormones disrupt almost all of the body's processes, increasing the risk of numerous health problems, including heart disease, sleep and stomach disorders, and depression.

Some also argue that inequality-linked stress impairs the production of a second hormone: oxytocin, sometimes called the "bonding hormone." According to research done at Stanford University and the University of Zurich, oxytocin is secreted during childbirth and breastfeeding and helps encourage healthy pair-bonding, trust, and other healthy social functions.

Studies by UCLA neuroscientist Naomi Eisenberger and others have demonstrated that certain social experiences are so psychologically painful that the human body regards them as physical pain – like putting your hand onto a burning flame. Eisenberger's neuroimaging studies have found that feelings of rejection and social exclusion were associated with activity in a brain region that is also involved in pain processing.

Working with neuroscientists from Harvard University and elsewhere through her non-profit Crittenton Women's Union, Elizabeth Babcock has highlighted how poverty-related situational stresses can alter young children's brain development. Growing up poor–with increased likelihood of chronic exposure to toxins, bad nutrition, prenatal drug use, feelings of exclusion and low social status, trauma, and often violence–can actually alter the brain's limbic system and prefrontal cortex, inhibiting impulse control, problem solving and executive functioning. Situational stress has even been shown to lower average IQ levels by a full standard deviation. In essence, poverty makes it more difficult for children to develop the very cognitive capacities and skills needed to compete and advance in the 21st century.

In short, poverty and inequality are actually a public health concern. Too bad, some argue. Life isn't fair. Inequality and poverty have always existed and always will. Perhaps so, but inequality in a democracy is simply bad public policy and ultimately bad business. There is overwhelming evidence that earlier public interventions in health and education can have a positive reinforcing economic impact. Getting kids into school earlier improves health and cognitive development, which helps them become better students, which helps boost enrollment and attainment rates. In turn, this should help increase productivity, competiveness, and incomes over time. Without policy interventions, poor areas like Watts will continue to exist side-by-side with more prosperous areas like Orange County. It would be far cheaper—and lead to a more globally competitive workforce—to invest earlier in human capital. Such an investment would ultimately reduce costs related to health care, unemployment, and crime.

Public Policy to the Rescue?

While there is an enormous amount of distrust in government today, public policy clearly has an impact on determining a country's socio-economic trajectory. Yes, Adam Smith's marketplace helps propel an economy forward, but it does not promote public schools or infrastructure; it cares little about pollution, food safety, or traffic; and it ignores income distribution. Only government can help complex societies with hundreds of millions of people function smoothly.

The difference between more successful and less successful countries? Years and years of solid public policy. Just as government stepped in with a new economic paradigm during the Great Depression, creating the GDP metric and implementing new fiscal policy, government can step in today to address economic challenges. To rebound strongly, America will need a radical shift to readdress the whole notion of public policy. As a democracy, America must codify the common good, using a paradigm that includes the best, most accurate information, rigorous analysis, and thoughtful policies.

If America started from scratch, all the while aware of its socioeconomic unevenness, would it base its national capacity to cultivate human capital on the price of real estate? As stated earlier, most public schools in the country are funded through property taxes, a problem unique to the U.S. Given that American schools are neither nationally nor state funded, unbundling public education funding from local property taxes has the potential to reduce the disparities in educational opportunities. It's clear America's "mortgage Keynesianism" policy, coupled with property-tax-based education, drove too much labor into the housing sector, forcing millions to take on trillions in excess debt. As a result, human capacities were neglected and the country's global competitiveness waned.

Some argue that the government shouldn't try to achieve more equitable distribution in society through social engineering; the market should determine that mix. Yes, market forces are important, but we forget that they are often driven by incentives that government policies shape. To that extent, public policies often pick winners and losers.

America's numerous legacy policy incentives have created a few billionaires while leaving countless citizens by the wayside.

When exploring the inherent biases in a country's political/economic system, it's helpful to start from scratch, from what American philosopher John Rawls called "the original position." To do so requires "a veil of ignorance," or lack of knowledge of incumbent differences in wealth and talent. Without knowing how society is *already* organized, we can then try to establish fair rules and incentives to optimize the benefits of social cooperation. So if you're an American, forget what zip code you were born into, or what position your parents held in society when you were born. Rawls directed us to consider society from the perspective of everyone in our democracy, including both the worst-off and best-off members.

If we adopt biases and incentives in public policy, Rawls asked, should they be for the top 10% or the bottom 10% of the country? His answer: the bottom 10%. They are the least advantaged, with the least capabilities and the least opportunities. It's tough to argue with this logic. Going forward, policies that acknowledge the relationships between workforce development, education, health, and the equality of capabilities will be critical in creating a more stable, prosperous America.

III

Brave New America:
Restoring Faith in Government
with Brave New Policies

In the opening episode of Aaron Sorkin's HBO series *The Newsroom*, a burned out TV anchorman named Will McAvoy sits on a panel at Northwestern University. "What makes America the greatest country in the world?" a student in the audience asks him. In a huff, he replies:

". . . *[T]here's absolutely no evidence to support the statement that we're the greatest country in the world. We're seventh in literacy, 27th in math, 22nd in science, 49th in life expectancy, 178th in infant mortality, third in median household income, number four in labor force, and number four in exports. We lead the world in only three categories: number of incarcerated citizens per capita, number of adults who believe angels are real, and defense spending, where we spend more than the next 26 countries combined, 25 of whom are allies.*

". . .*[America] sure used to be. We stood up for what was right. We fought for moral reason. We passed laws, struck down laws, for moral reason. We waged wars on poverty, not on poor people. We sacrificed, we cared about our neighbors, we put our money where our mouths were, and we never beat our chest. We built great, big things, made ungodly technological advances, explored the universe, cured diseases, and we cultivated the world's greatest artists and the world's greatest economy. We reached for the stars, acted like men. We aspired to intelligence, we didn't belittle it. It didn't make us feel inferior. We didn't identify ourselves by who we voted for in the last election, and we didn't scare so easy. We were able to be all these things and do all these things because we were*

*informed . . . by great men, men who were revered. First step in
solving any problem is recognizing there is one. America is not
the greatest country in the world anymore."*

Sorkin's observations reflect the sentiments of many Americans.
While his numbers may be off, and he romantically glosses over many
downsides in old America, such as the oppression of women and
minorities, his character's rant touches on much of what we've already
discussed. Though America's GDP remains the largest in the world,
our public policies have let us down in many ways.

While Adam Smith's marketplace satisfies many needs, it can't do
everything. It can't provide a strong military, ensure robust public
education and public health, or protect the environment. These are jobs
for government, and only government has the muscle to dramatically
shape an economy. Despite being the piñata of talk radio, government
cannot be underestimated when it comes to major societal change.

For much of the 20th century, public policies in a number of areas,
including defense, health, agriculture, and information technology,
enabled America to lead the world not just in specific technologies but
in entire industries. Aircraft, radar, satellite and GPS, digital imaging,
the Internet, computers, microwaves—all were launched and supported
by government programs. Government has, and should continue, to be
the single greatest catalyst in American society.

So if we ask the question, "How can America become the greatest
country in the world again?" There is only one answer: public policy.
Much as socioeconomic development was once guided by the formation
of GDP and the application of fiscal stimulus programs like the Works
Projects Administration, prosperity today is best achieved through a
broad range of new public policies. While this seems unlikely at a time
when the nation's capital is so dysfunctional, the markets alone cannot
mobilize America to reach for the stars again. Only government can.

If you don't believe in the power of government, just visit China.
One of the world's poorest countries a generation ago, China has
engineered an economic miracle in a few short decades. Along with
implementing dozens of public policies designed to reduce poverty
and increase human capacity, China has built as much new

infrastructure as all the other world's emerging countries combined. China's economy is now the second largest in the world, based on nominal GDP. When evaluated on the basis of purchasing power parity (PPP), China's GDP grew from less than $250 billion in 1980 to more than $12 trillion in 2012. Globally, China skyrocketed from accounting for only 2% of the world economy to more than 15%. On the human capital side, the country had only 50,000 people in college in the late 1970s, when its population was roughly one billion. Today? More than 25 million people in China are enrolled in college, about seven million more than are enrolled in America.

We can talk at length about how and why China has risen, but the fact is that the Chinese government set objectives and radically changed public policy to enhance the capabilities of its people, to improve the country's public infrastructure, and to participate and compete in the global economy. In contrast, India is perhaps a generation behind China in terms of air, sea, rail, and road infrastructure, and its population is only 76% literate, compared to 96% in China. That's about 250 million less literate people. In this respect, the world can learn something from China. We can also follow a cue from the Social Science Research Council: investment in people's capacities is critical, as is the building and maintenance of a nation's infrastructure. The Invisible Hand can only work when it's part of a strong body of public policies.

Policy Area #1: Brave New Information

Within the U.S. federal government, as well as state and local governments, most agencies tasked with monitoring America's complex 21st-century economy have struggled to provide integrated data. Andrew Reamer of the Brookings Institution and George Washington University notes, "[The] U.S. has lacked a coherent, integrated policy for addressing competitive vulnerabilities ... [Its] approach to policy remains in a mid-20th-century macroeconomic policy framework." Akin to a *Moneyball*-type sabermetrician in D.C. circles, Reamer has called on government to embrace and develop more sophisticated and broader measures to guide public policies.

In the U.S., the numbers are compiled largely by three agencies in different cabinet departments: the Census Bureau, the Bureau of Economic Analysis, and the Bureau of Labor Statistics. Together, they are allotted a two to three thousand employees and approximately $2 billion of Washington's $3.7 trillion budget to study America's complicated $16 trillion GDP economy. Is American labor truly productive? And with which countries does America really run trade surpluses and deficits? Given the country's antiquated methodology and the agencies' small resources, it's tough to say—and that's embarrassing in the Information Age. It's also dangerous.

Reamer has testified before Congress and written many papers detailing America's numerous weaknesses: an overreliance on error-prone manual compilation; a lack of definition standards among agencies, which results in inconsistent data quality; redundant efforts to extract and publish data in multiple places and for multiple purposes without leveraging the proper instruments or understanding; and, most importantly, poor communication and information sharing between agencies. Reamer, along with dozens of other academics, also believes that America's three primary information bureaus need to work more closely with the Internal Revenue Service to create massive data pools for more detailed analyses on labor, sectors, geography, income, and education, particularly their inter-linkages.

Our first brave new recommendation, then, is to create a cabinet level Department of Information (DoI), whose secretary will function similarly to a chief information officer at a large company. This DoI would oversee the creation and management of a data warehouse that could serve as a central resource, not only for the federal government but also for state and local governments. At the risk of looking like Big Brother, all the current major information centers would be folded into this agency. In addition to generating proprietary information, the DoI would, in partnership with private data suppliers, rely on timely market information and surveys of both objective and subjective measurements of well-being to begin broader, deeper analyses than ever before. As a result, the government would be able to see how policies affect society faster, allowing for better information loops and refined policies. Additionally, the data warehouse would be globalized so analysts and academics alike could track socio-economic trends around the world in an effort to better understand America's global connections and global competiveness.

Who knows what would be discovered. In the area of labor, for example, data from the payroll company ADP, job listings on Monster.com, or domestic and international news websites have the potential to provide more valuable insights into employment than simple phone interviews and unemployment benefit data alone. Moreover, all labor linked data could be tested and regressed with world trends, helping government to develop some predictive skills on how rising education in Asia, new industries in Latin America, or migration from Africa will affect jobs in the U.S. or elsewhere.

Already the private sector is attempting to harness Big Data for predictive capabilities in the economics arena. The Billions Prices Project at MIT, for example, is exploring ways to use real-time information for inflation forecasting. As opposed to having hundreds or thousands of people out checking prices, MIT professors use computer scripts and information from the private firm PriceStats, which analyzes thousands of e-commerce websites. The MIT project hopes to determine what drives price stickiness around the world, how price swings among thousands of goods and services are linked, how prices adjust when exchange rates or commodity prices fluctuate, and how regional prices vary according to countries, regions, cities, and even zip codes. In addition to helping economists construct better baskets, this information, unlike that gleaned from the blunt and less informative CPI, could lead to a far richer understanding of true inflation and purchasing power.

Local vs. National Economies?

In this brave new world, growing evidence suggests that the U.S. government would benefit greatly from mining regional and local data to understand how these subset economies fare relative to others in the country. There are many social scientists who believe it no longer makes sense to craft national economic policy in complex countries like the U.S. or China. Instead, we must think of a national economy as an assemblage of regional economies within a larger global system. As social scientist Richard Florida notes:

> *Nations have long been considered the fundamental economic units of the world, but that distinction no longer holds true. Today, the natural units—and engines—of the global economy are megaregions, cities and suburbs in powerful conurbations, at times spanning national borders, forming vast swaths of trade, transport, innovation, and talent. The world economy is organized around a few dozen megaregions—areas like the Boston-New York-Washington corridor, or the Shanghai-Nanjing-Hangzhou triangle, or the span stretching from London through Leeds, Manchester, Liverpool, and into Birmingham—which account for the bulk of the globe's economic activity and innovation.*

Florida has identified some 42 global megaregions in advanced and emerging markets that comprise less than 18% of the world's population but account for two-thirds of global economic activity and more than 83% of scientific research and patent innovations. He uses a brave new measurement—satellite images of the world at night—to derive a systematic measure of economic output based on light or energy emissions. He calls his new measurement Light-Based Regional Product (LRP, calculated in U.S. dollars). While examining LRPs, which, when viewed from satellite, don't show city, state, or national borders, Florida rightly notes that it's misleading to think of America as a single national economy or even as 50 individual state economies.

In reality, America's economic activity occurs within a dozen megaregions on the East and West Coasts, with some smaller ones in the heartland. The famous I-95 corridor of Boston-NY-Washington alone boasts 50 million people and produces roughly 15% of America's economic activity—more than the UK or French national economies. Europe, too, is made up of megaregions, the largest running from Amsterdam and Rotterdam through Belgium, France, and into Germany. This megaregion has almost 60 million people and an LRP of $1.5 trillion—larger than all of Canada.

In emerging markets, the Mexico City region is home to more than 45 million people and has an LRP of $290 billion, more than half of Mexico's total. In Brazil, the Rio de Janeiro to São Paulo corridor produces an LRP of $230 billion, more than 40% of Brazil's LRP, and is home to 43 million people. Three megaregions along China's east coast have been found to be the major engines of what is now the world's second largest economy in GDP terms. Indeed, Florida has found that megaregions are the growth engines of emerging economies. The large disparities between industrialized cities and towns in these emerging economies too, can lead to Swiss cheese national economies with empty pockets next to full ones.

According to Florida, megaregions have been successful in attracting and cultivating what he calls his "3Ts"—talent, technology, and tolerance—which foster greater, sustainable economic activity. He's created several new indices which examine data from LRPs relative to 3Ts, including scholarly publications, patents, gay and artist populations, and education levels that promote creativity, economic activity, and increased productivity. Parag Khanna has suggested a similar league table idea in an effort for cities to compete for talent and boost their economies.

Innovative studies by Geoffrey West and researchers at Hanover University are investigating "economic metabolism" – borrowing models from physics and biology - and what can accelerate it in cities and regions. At New York University, Paul Romer has been advocating "charter cities" – started from scratch – utilizing best policy practices conducive for faster growth in smaller geographies.

If the U.S. government studied economic activity at the city or regional levels, and if one-size-fits-all policies were eschewed in favor of smaller programs, sustainable economic activity would be easier to initiate locally. In fact, such an approach has the potential to unlock and transform our understanding of economic dynamics, which in turn could lead to the design and implementation of customized solutions for different regions with different people and capacities.

We're already seeing Big Data help some fairly large cities (and economies) function better and improve well-being outside of GDP. In New York City, former Mayor Michael Bloomberg's Office of Policy and Strategic Planning now sifts through one terabyte of information each day—the equivalent of 143 million printed pages—including *Twitter* and *Facebook* feeds and blogs posts. For a modest $1 million investment, Bloomberg's in-house geek squad has harnessed the power of computers in a wide range of activities, including doubling NYC's success rate in identifying stores that sell bootleg cigarettes, detecting which restaurants flush grease down sinks and cause sewage problems, speeding up the removal of trees destroyed by Hurricane Sandy, pinpointing specific locations of drug trafficking, better understanding crime patterns, and helping identify code-violating buildings where catastrophic fires are likeliest to occur.

In Chicago, Mayor Rahm Emmanuel and his chief technology officer John Tolva have consolidated reams of data at metrochicagodata.org, a convergence cloud that provides for business and citizens a huge amount of information, from dynamic crime maps, towed vehicles, current car traffic patterns, and snow plowing progress to current city budget breakdowns. All this saves time and money—and actually improves the way government works—while establishing greater transparency and building trust with citizens. Notwithstanding their obvious value, however, these improvements in the quality of American life are not necessarily captured in GDP terms.

Faster Computing, and Make it Snappy!

With the task of analyzing more data than ever before, one of the first charges of our new Department of Information will be to deploy greater computing power. In order to harness Big Data, we will need massive exascale supercomputing capabilities at speeds of a thousand times our fastest computing today. In the future, exascale can and will be used in almost all commercial activities and public initiatives, from solving climate change to finding new renewable energy sources (like fusion). It will also be used in the health and defense industries. Exascale computing has the potential to be our first "race to the moon" in the 21st century, and government will be needed to accelerate the process.

Of course, exascale computing will come with its own requirements. The energy needs of supercomputing are substantial. To effectively use such technology, we'll need massive cooling stations to keep exascale computers online, and this may strain our current electricity infrastructure. While the U.S. has the huge advantage of some of the cheapest electricity in the world, it will need more and more reliable power grids as many businesses increasingly rely on supercomputing and cloud computing. Big Data requires big energy.

We're only at the beginning of the Big Data revolution, but it's clear that we'll ultimately need to change the culture of policymaking to include a wider array of information and social activity. This paradigm shift will free us from GDP-anchored policy, and only government can be the engine of this revolution.

Policy Area #2: Brave New Education

New York Times columnist Thomas Friedman, in his book *The World Is Flat*, declared that no one could afford to be average anymore:

> *In the past, workers with average skills, doing an average job, could earn an average lifestyle. But, today, average is officially over. Being average just won't earn you what it used to. It can't when so many more employers have so much more access to so much more above average cheap foreign labor, cheap robotics, cheap software, cheap automation, and cheap genius. Therefore, everyone needs to find their extra—their unique value contribution that makes them stand out in whatever is their field of employment. Average is over.*

It's no coincidence that rising opportunities in formal education have paralleled the globalizing economy. Mass primary and secondary education has created an extraordinary explosion in human capital and output, not only in wealthy places like the U.S., West Europe, and Japan, but also in the developing countries of Asia, Africa, the Middle East, and Latin America. World supply chains that make iPods and Mini Coopers have been built upon capable workers, new information and communication technologies, and pro-market philosophies that engage more countries and people in producing more goods and services than ever before.

As Bill Gates told Tom Friedman in *The World Is Flat*, if you had to choose between being a genius born in Shanghai or an average person born in Poughkeepsie in 1980, you would have chosen Poughkeepsie because your chances of living a better life were much greater in America than in China. "Now," Bill Gates says, "I would rather be a genius born in China than an average guy born in Poughkeepsie." It's true. Globalization has "flattened" the world, and American human capital now competes with human capital everywhere 24/7.

In a globalized world without borders, educating and improving human capital should be America's Public Policy Number 1. To stay competitive, the U.S. needs a "knowledge economy"—a greater reliance on brainpower to do things better in almost every sector. Americans can no longer expect to increase their living standards by sewing gloves or flipping burgers. As the so-called "Smiling Curve" of Added Value illustrates below, there are only "thin" profits to be had in labor-intensive industries such as assembly and basic manufacturing. "Thick" profits, on the other hand, require higher-level skill sets, and that means better and more education.

Figure 15.

The "Smiling Curve" of Added Value in Industry

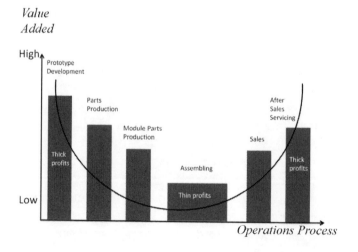

Indeed, as the global economy evolves and technology grows more complex, the need for higher-skilled labor has certainly increased. In their 2008 book, *The Race Between Education and Technology,* Harvard Professors Claudia Goldin and Lawrence Katz offer an elegant explanation: until the 1970s, America did a decent job of educating its populace (with the exceptions of certain minorities) in order to keep pace with technological advances and provide a broad dispersion of the country's economic gains. But sometime during the 1970s and 1980s, American education began to lose the race with technology, such that skill advancement no longer occurred in the same broad-based way across the country. Those lucky enough to keep pace with the new skills began to see wage gaps increase between them and those who hadn't kept pace. In fact, this phenomenon helped foster the growing inequality in the country. As we mentioned earlier, one-quarter of Americans haven't been finishing high school for more than a generation; they clearly have been left behind. Such an analysis is confirmed by French economists Thomas Picketty and Emmanuel Saez, who have analyzed American inequality trends over the last century. Likewise, the OECD's *Economic Survey of the United States* recently noted American demand for university-educated workers has outstripped supply for a generation now—long enough that U.S. companies are no longer more likely to innovate than companies in the other 33 OECD member countries. This is in stark contrast to some 40 years ago.

While formal education is clearly linked to more income and social mobility, growing evidence demonstrates that more educated people are actually happier and more creative on many levels. Countless studies show that higher education is strongly related to open-mindedness and key values like tolerance to diversity. Such values, if fostered at a national level, could cultivate what Peter Drucker called a "knowledge society" mindset—with many benefits. For example, one of the most important things we can take away from a formal education is the understanding that there are many ways to be happy and pursue the good life—and not all are about material wealth.

Ample evidence demonstrates the positive links between education and occupational status, health, and marital status. Individuals with higher levels of education often work in occupations and fields that require greater levels of cognitive and social skill, and studies of job satisfaction note a close connection between more challenging work and overall happiness. A variety of studies have also underscored that crime, dependence on governmental assistance, and other stresses on community resources generally decline as education levels rise. Sociologists, economists, and psychologists often debate which comes first—wealth, education, or health—but the truth is that they are all interconnected in a virtuous circle and should be nurtured and encouraged simultaneously. The links between education and general well-being are both intuitive and statistical. America, therefore, must prioritize education while crafting public policy.

Below are five brave new policy suggestions that have the potential to put the U.S. back on the right educational path:

1. Brave New Information and Benchmarking. One of the first things Americans need is better information and benchmarking in U.S. education. In addition to forming our new DoI, we need to earmark more funds to the Department of Education to reinforce its stated mission of promoting "student achievement and preparation for global competitiveness by fostering educational excellence and ensuring equal access." A modest increase in funding for more and better statistics and benchmarking could yield improved insights and policies by better understanding what works and what doesn't.

Stanford's Eric Hanushek, in his seminal research, has demonstrated the strong statistical correlation between the quality of a country's school system and its economic growth. There are strong links to high test scores on PISA (Program for International Student Assessment) exams and a country's economic gains over time. Likewise, more education generates higher labor productivity. Simply stated, boosting PISA scores and lengthening the time spent in school would have a long-lasting impact on human capabilities—and thus national well-being. And American PISA scores have been lagging for more than a generation. Now, how to improve scores is debatable, but the first task is to keep better track of the American education system—not just averages but the broader distribution of quality in all zip codes. What do we need to monitor better? Everything.

The World Bank's Knowledge Economy Index and ranking system includes dozens of statistics that show America's level of education and attainment, but for our task we need to better understand regional and local differences. As with income, we don't want our educational picture skewed by structural disparities. As the Social Science Research Council notes, the top five states in their Education Index spent more than $14,500 per K–12 pupil. The bottom five spent less than $9,000 per pupil. In California's Thirtieth Congressional District (Hollywood, Beverly Hills, Santa Monica, and Malibu), nearly three in five adult residents are college graduates, and more than one in four have advanced degrees. A few miles west in California's District 34 (downtown Los Angeles), only three in 100 residents have advanced degrees.

2. More Schooling, Reoriented Calendars. The U.S. public education system is a vestige of the 18th century, a time when 85% of Americans were involved in agriculture and schools lacked air conditioners. Who says the American system should only be from kindergarten through 12th grade? And why does the U.S. follow the current calendar, with long breaks in the summer?

In the age of information and globalization, the U.S. must create better students by starting public education at a much earlier age. Two influential studies from Harvard University underscore the neuroscience of early childhood development, noting the formation of some 700 neuron connections every second in the first few years of life. According to such research, without sufficient nurturing, nutrition, and stimulation during those early years, a child's ability to learn and thrive is severely impaired. As a result, the child's learning ability could be stunted in the long run. Indeed, the income level that someone is born into now increasingly determines the economic and health trajectory of that person's life. This is sad but true: children who are deprived—both economically and socially—routinely enter kindergarten already "left behind." Many studies note that wide economic disparities and problems in later life could be alleviated with earlier interventions through education. As former Undersecretary of Education Linus Wright observes:

> *What if all children during their very early years were given the tools to be successful in the school environment? They would be better able to make good choices, follow a productive path, and have greater chance of success in their college years. As a matter of economic policy, this change could substantially reduce expenses, at all levels, associated with remedial education and student dropouts—not to mention potential longer-term savings in reduced welfare, incarceration, and Medicaid costs.*

By mandating full-day public education for all three- and four-year-olds, Americans could begin cultivating human capital at a much earlier stage. How could this be paid for? Wright suggests eliminating the 12th grade. He argues that it's the least productive and most expensive of all school years, and the money saved by eliminating it would cover more robust early-childhood programs, which have proven to be the most productive and least expensive. There is a snowball effect, with students gaining momentum over time, thereby improving PISA scores and high school graduation rates. With better students at the 11th grade level, many would be far better prepared to move on to higher education—and not simply four years of residential college.

We should also consider more school days per annum—and shorter summer vacations. Data suggest that prolonged summer breaks of eight to 10 weeks actually lead to learning loss and the need for re-teaching. American students would fare better with three four-week breaks spread out more evenly through the year. Improving student capabilities over a lifetime would also help to increase college completion rates. Even at the community college level, some 50% of U.S. students require remedial education and have difficulties completing programs.

3. Wider Range of Higher Education. If formal high school ended at 11th grade, more education would be needed for the U.S. to remain globally competitive. While most people believe that a four-year degree is the best path to the middle-class, Carnevale notes that there are some 29 million jobs in America that pay middle-class wages but don't actually require a four-year degree. That's not to say they don't require more "education." On the contrary, Carnevale notes five learning pathways that lead to these jobs, including (1) employer-based training, (2) industry-based certifications, (3) apprenticeships, (4) postsecondary certificates from colleges, and (5) associate's degrees. The OECD has also echoed many of these suggestions.

The vast, largely untapped U.S. community college system, which includes more than 1,200 institutions spread throughout the country and across the most remote towns and villages, would benefit greatly from many of Carnevale's recommendations. In fact, a recent U.S. Census study noted that two-year technical degrees often paid more than many bachelor degrees in non-technical fields. Unfortunately, labs and technology equipment cost money, and federal government funding for these institutions is currently modest, with most monies going to public four-year schools. Part of the solution lies in tying into local and regional businesses to create incentives for more cooperative educational programs. Local governments and colleges, in combination with state and federal incentives, can encourage potential employers to tailor programs to the needs of the local job market. In addition, federal funding incentives can promote relationships among community colleges, regional technical schools, other postsecondary institutions, and employers to build more cooperative style schooling that includes internships and work programs, similar to those found in Germany and Switzerland.

4. Cheaper Four-Year Degrees. As Carnevale and others have noted, America hasn't been graduating enough students with four-year bachelor's degrees. According to the OECD, graduation rates for America's older generation (55 to 64) and the younger generation (25 to 34) are flat—at 40%—while in many other OECD countries the younger generation far surpasses the older generation. The plateau in

U.S. college completion rates contrasts sharply with gains in emerging markets, which send more students to college, including some 800,000 each year to American schools. This is another piece of America's economic stagnation puzzle: the U.S. has been educationally stagnant for a long time while others have caught up. And, yes, America still educates many people beyond high school, but the lack of higher penetration rates has contributed to a less competitive, less stable economy.

There are two frequently cited reasons for failing to raise U.S. college completion rates: poor preparation and exploding cost. The first may be fixable with some of the suggestions above. Improving students' ability to learn through earlier education certainly has the potential to help student preparedness. Moreover, steering people away from four-year tracks toward one of Carnevale's five suggested pathways would also reduce dropout rates.

While college costs have outpaced inflation for decades in the U.S., there are other changes that could be implemented to curb such growth. Online education, a promising development in this regard, can be harnessed to dramatically revamp the cost structure of traditional residential colleges. One of the largest costs of American schools is their bricks and mortar. The U.S. residential college system is unique. With the exception of a few universities worldwide, most colleges are largely urban. The 500-acre suburban campus with rolling fields and beautiful quads and fraternity houses, while appealing, is something of a luxury. Niceties like dorms and sports stadiums all cost money and have only a peripheral impact on education.

We are still in the early days of online technology, but increasing evidence suggests that solid programming can be delivered over the Internet. While advertising from for-profit online and hybrid schools like the University of Phoenix is ubiquitous, schools such as Western Governor's University have been able to develop a reputable online bachelor's degree and bring down tuition to roughly $6,000 per annum. The University of Texas is also exploring ways to lower the cost of a four-year degree to less than $20,000—half the average cost of one year of private college tuition—with a combination of online and in-person delivery. In 2013, Georgia Tech began offering an online master's degree in computer science for a remarkable $7,000, which is a fraction of the cost of comparable residential degrees. As soon as Americans abandon the notion of "going off to college" and see higher education as merely advanced learning, the U.S. can begin to develop more cost-efficient ways to deliver it to more people. Online technology undoubtedly will be part of this cost solution. Tom Friedman has also suggested compressing bachelors' degrees to only three years (with less vacation time). This is closer to the time allotted for similar degrees in Europe and elsewhere and could reduce expenses, as well.

5. Eliminate Property Tax-based Public Education. In the U.S., property taxes have largely financed public education, which relies on very little federal funding, and this uneven approach has clearly shaped much of the American experience for a century. As discussed earlier, wealthy zip codes spend more on quality education, thereby reinforcing America's socio-economic divide. This in turn feeds into social anxiety at all levels of society.

If it was possible to start with a blank slate, the U.S., after looking to the rest of the world for examples on how to fund public education, would likely institute state and federal funding, which would create a far more even system. For those wishing to opt out of the public system, there would still be private alternatives. But as part of a larger tax overhaul we'll discuss later, rebalancing public education funding away from property taxes and toward state and federal sources has the potential to improve human capacities and close massive socio-economic gaps in American society. While this may seem politically impossible, one could envision a gradual elimination and rebalance implemented over, say, a 30-year period.

Policy Area #3: Brave New Immigration

Immigration, long a fountainhead for American innovation, entrepreneurship, and human talent, has become a dirty word in the U.S., connoting illegal aliens stealing jobs. It's a political quandary, too, since the benefits of immigration are widely dispersed, and opposition is largely driven by emotion. Immigrants don't vote in elections, and citizens who do vote see immigration as a threat. Politicians, therefore, have little incentive to address, much less solve, the problem.

This is unfortunate, because strategically conceived and well-targeted immigration could be a precision tool for providing America with just the right mix of human capabilities to compete in the 21st century. The educational recommendations above would certainly help in the long run, but in the short run, new highly skilled immigrants represent the quickest bang for virtually no bucks.

Let's also not forget that some of the most hallowed names in American business and technology—from Andrew Carnegie and Alexander Graham Bell in the late 19th century to Sergey Brin and Elon Musk in the 21st century—came to America as immigrants. Indeed, some studies estimate that immigrants have founded 50% of Fortune 500 companies and 25% of all new small U.S. businesses.

Immigrants continue contribute trillions of dollars annually to the U.S. economy, helping stratify labor, as well as injecting some entrepreneurial spirit to the country. This is important to remember, even while millions of Americans are out of work, because immigration is not a zero sum game that takes one job from an American for every immigrant hired. To the contrary, the numbers suggest that immigrants increase job opportunities for all Americans.

But the U.S. has competition for talent again, remember Wriston's Law. While America used to be the best place in the world to become rich and successful, several developing countries have built fast growing economies in the last 30 years. Along with China, dozens of emerging markets now offer talented individuals the potential to make their dreams come true in their home countries. Indeed, the *Forbes* 2013 list of 1426 billionaires included 442 Americans (some of foreign descent) but also 386 Asians, 129 from Latin America, and 96 each from Russia and 103 from the Middle East and Africa. And these numbers are likely conservative. Forbes calculates net worth in U.S. dollar terms, adjusting for PPP and undervalued currencies in emerging markets, which means there are probably many more billionaires (and millions of millionaires) in developing countries that did not exist back in Communist China and the former Soviet Union.

As discussed earlier, official unemployment in the U.S. stood below 8% in late 2013, but America is still critically short of skilled professionals. While the global economy has evolved, U.S. immigration laws haven't changed much since 1990, which is why high-tech giants like Bill Gates and the late Steve Jobs testified before Congress in support of issuing more visas to foreign students and scientists for Science Technology Engineering and Math (STEM) fields. In fact, in April 2013, Facebook founder Mark Zuckerberg and other tech titans helped found FWD.US, an initiative to push for comprehensive immigration reform to help attract talent to the country. And the reality is that Silicon Valley needs this brainpower. According to Manpower Inc., the U.S. ranked fifth highest globally in talent shortages, with 49% of employers surveyed experiencing critical problems. The average among industrialized countries, by comparison, is much lower at 34%.

Beyond the shortages in STEM professionals, America faces an aging workforce, thanks in particular to the rapid retirement of the Baby Boom generation. To maintain a balanced and a stable labor pool, U.S. businesses must find younger workers, especially for lower-skilled jobs. With more and more Americans earning college degrees and aspiring to white-collar professions, filling jobs in certain sectors is becoming extremely difficult, even in this tough economy. At the lower end of the labor pool, industries like agriculture require a large workforce ready, willing, and able to work long and physically demanding days. Since the beginning of the 20th century, such sectors have relied on immigrant workers to do these jobs. Hotels, restaurants, business services, and certain manufacturing sectors face similar problems, which will only intensify as Americans age, making immigration central to keeping the U.S. economy diversified and competitive.

There's plenty of room in America for more people. The U.S. has one of the lowest population densities in the world at approximately 85 people per square mile. Compare this to China at 360, India at more than 900, Japan at 875, Germany near 600, and the UK at 650. Many

American cities, which have actually depopulated in the last 30 years, have ample infrastructure to accommodate new families and skilled workers. New Orleans, Detroit, Cleveland, Rochester, and Buffalo, among others, have lost thousands of people yet still offer big city infrastructure, education, and opportunities. Moreover, since the financial crisis, the U.S. has an excess of housing that is ready to be absorbed. Targeted immigration policies could be meshed with special economic zones and other incentives to revive cities, satisfy skill gaps, and restore greater long-term stability and competitiveness to American labor markets.

As of early 2013, five brave new immigration policies have been endorsed by many non-partisan groups in the U.S. Each is worth considering:

1. Raising H-1B Caps. The H-1B temporary high-skilled visa is often the only option for foreign-born STEM graduates who want to stay in the U.S. and work on cutting-edge research at American firms. But arbitrary caps on H-1Bs set during the Bush Administration, currently set at 65,000 per year, fill quickly. In 2003, the limit was 195,000. The U.S. could easily ramp this up to 250,000 while implementing some of the suggestions below. It could also expand the categories in which no cap applies—as is now the case for research jobs. Moreover, the U.S. should make it easier for skilled immigrants on H-1B visas to apply for permanent residency once their temporary visas expire. This issue is particularly acute for workers from countries like China and India, which now overwhelm per-country visa caps. Indeed, adjusting per-country green card limits would help to address this problem.

2. Automatic Residency for Targeted Graduates. Another way to fine-tune the American workforce would be to target specific skilled foreign graduates at U.S. schools. One of America's greatest success stories has been its unrivalled research universities. In 2013, the Institute of International Education's "Open Doors" report noted that a record high 819,644 foreign students are now studying for degrees in the U.S. For decades American schools have trained some of the world's top innovators and, too often, sent them back home to compete against the U.S. in the global marketplace.

To keep this talent, these human capabilities, the U.S. should grant green cards to foreign students who earn STEM and other advanced degrees at American schools. Why not keep this American-educated talent? This might also encourage more gifted foreign students to come to U.S. universities and supply them with needed revenue. Foreigners studying in America already contribute more than $20 billion in annual revenues, but this number could easily double given the vast size of the U.S. university system. This is a unique "export" in which America still has a comparative advantage. American schools dominate approximately 60% of world university rankings. Attracting the best and brightest by offering them the potential to live in the U.S. could pay significant economic dividends for a generation or more.

3. Targeted Residency for Health Care Professionals. According to the Association of American Medical Colleges, a doctor shortage in the U.S. was expected even before the 2010 Affordable Care Act made millions of additional people eligible for health care coverage. Current shortages are projected to grow to 90,000 by 2020 but may reach nearly 150,000 by the end of the next decade. Doctors require years of education and cannot be trained quickly. Nurses, too, are in short supply. A partial solution would be to increase nursing and medical schools as part of a larger brave new health care initiative (see below), but this will take time. According to the American Association of Colleges of Nursing, for example, in 2010 there were 67,000 qualified applicants for nursing programs rejected due to shortages in faculty. Nevertheless, immigration of skilled health care has the potential to dramatically relieve shortages over the near term.

4. Entrepreneur Visas. Immigrants are often resourceful and help make a country more innovative. As mentioned above, immigrant founders represent 25% of public venture-backed U.S. companies. Yet sadly, there is no U.S. visa for foreign-born entrepreneurs who want to start companies and employ American workers. The current investor visa requires evidence that a business is already well established, creating a chicken-versus-egg problem. Notwithstanding this, new proposed legislation, the Startup Visa Act of 2013 would provide visas to individuals while requiring a minimum number of jobs created and certain revenue minimums after a period of time. This is a great idea that shouldn't be bogged down in politics.

5. Revamp Low-Skilled Immigration. The economic role of low-skilled immigrants is the most controversial in the immigration debate. Many in the U.S. view these low-skilled workers as economic leeches who steal American jobs, particularly during hard times. But this view misses the essence of comparative advantage and underestimates how such workers contribute to the U.S. economy. Low-skilled workers help stratify labor, enabling Americans to specialize in more productive sectors. Consider office assistants, who allow doctors to see more patients; or construction workers, who free engineers and architects to focus on their specialties; or child care providers, who free mothers and fathers to work. They all contribute to a mobile, dynamic American workforce that can specialize and compete in the global economy.

Many criticize low-skilled, low-paid immigrants because they pay little in federal income taxes. But we forget that it's not just these low-income immigrants who don't pay federal income tax. According to the Internal Revenue Service, some 46% of all Americans had no income tax liability in 2012. But, as many studies note, these workers contribute billions in sales and payroll taxes *and* promote broader growth.[6] In addition, those paying income taxes using "borrowed" Social Security numbers pay billions of dollars in payroll taxes each year that they will never be able to withdraw as Social Security benefits. The overall effect is more sales, and more sales helps economies of scale and efficiency, which lowers per-unit costs for businesses and prices for consumers. Immigration even at the low end, therefore, allows consumers to spend, save, and invest more, which

---

[6] See the excellent 2011 study by Georgetown University's Harry Holzer, *Immigration Policy and Less-Skilled Workers in the United States: Reflections on Future Directions for Reform.*

leads to more taxable economic activity that benefits America as a whole.

In addition to implementing the higher-end immigration reforms mentioned above, the U.S. should allow lower-skilled workers on employment-based visas to switch employers more easily and gain a path to citizenship. America should also lower visa fees and streamline the process to make it less costly for employers to hire such workers. A 2010 study by the Center for American Progress and Immigration Policy Center makes a compelling economic argument for comprehensive immigration reform that would include legalization and a path to citizenship for currently undocumented workers. Over 10 years, the study contends, such a reform would add $1.5 trillion to the U.S. economy. If these same people were to be deported, on the other hand, it would cost the U.S. $2.6 trillion in reduced economic activity.

Immigration reform in the U.S. means acknowledging the competition for labor globally—and the fact that America is no longer the only economic game in town. Australia, Canada, Ireland, the UK, and Singapore, among others, have eased their visa processes to entice foreign students, innovators, and entrepreneurs. If U.S. politicians don't reform the country's antiquated immigration system soon, America risks jeopardizing its ability to attract talented foreigners, to leverage its comparative advantage in research universities, and to continue to innovate. America's success has always hinged on cultivating productive human capital, and brave new immigration is an important part of keeping its global edge.

Policy Area #4: Brave New Health

America is a vast land, but in the end, it's made up of people—more than 300 million—and their capabilities. The increased health and wellness of people should be the principal goal of government. It certainly is in terms of the economy. Health care costs now comprise approximately 20% of America's $16+ trillion (and counting) GDP.

Health and wellness deserve even more thoughtful public policy as life expectancy has expanded in a relatively short period of time. When I was born in the mid-1960s, the average American could expect to live about 70 years (about 67 for men, 73 for women), which at the time was one of the highest rates in the world. By 2000, this had risen to 77 years (74 and 80 respectively). The lengthening of life has dramatically redefined the human experience and requires us to think and plan differently than we did a century ago. Planning means determining how we'll work and for how long. It means calculating how to save for longer retirement needs. Many of America's financial problems with Social Security, Medicare, and pension plans (both private and public plans) stem from a mid-20th-century information failure to predict how long Americans will live.

As a species, we have an incredibly poor track record of forecasting our own life expectancy. In the late 1920s, L.I. Dublin, the chief actuary of the Metropolitan Life Insurance Company, capped life expectancy at 64.75 years for both men and women. A decade later in the 1930s, he collaborated with a mathematician to revise this to 69.93 years. More recently, a leading gerontologist set an upper limit on life (barring some major breakthrough in molecular biology) of 85 +/- 7 years.

Nobel laureate Robert Fogel wrote that these caps tend to be five to 10 years beyond the observed life expectancy at the time of the forecasts. Based on technological improvements and lifestyle changes, Fogel predicted that female life expectancy should increase a little more than two years per decade: by 2070 female life expectancy in America should rise to between 92.5 and 101.5 years, substantially higher than the Social Security Administration's forecast of 83.9.

Longer life expectancy could have significant costs if thoughtful, data-driven policy decisions aren't made soon. The "fiscal cliff" debates of 2012 and 2013 exposed the runaway costs of Medicare and other future federal liabilities like Social Security. Over the long term, Medicare and Social Security could explode as America grows old and faces a decreasing ratio of workers to retirees. According to the Center for Medicare and Medicaid Services, total Medicare spending from 2010 to 2020 is projected to jump 80%, from $523 billion to $932 billion. From 2010 to 2030, Medicare enrollment is expected to rise from 47 million to 79 million people, with a declining ratio of workers to enrollees from 3.7 to 2.4. And if we project outward several decades, Medicare spending is expected to increase from 3.6% of GDP in 2010 to 5.6% in 2035 and 6.2% by 2080.

While it's true that Americans are living longer, the U.S. ranks around 50th in the world in life expectancy at 78.5 years. Canada (81.5), Australia (81.9), and Japan (83.91) each rank higher, and this three-to-five-year shortfall between the U.S. and some of its peer countries is a significant difference in biological terms. By many other statistical measures, the U.S. health system compares poorly with other countries. Americans suffer high rates of disease that are self-inflicted, thanks to decades of overconsumption. Such overconsumption helped GDP expand for decades—and will continue to do so through years of remediation. America has one of the highest daily caloric intakes in the world at roughly 3,750, which is 1,000 more than the intake of the Japanese, who live, on average, five years longer than Americans.

Far from a healthy country, the U.S. has the world's highest obesity rate: approximately 30.6% of the population, which is several points ahead of the next highest country. In contrast, Canada has only a 14.3% obesity rate. According to the International Diabetes Foundation, approximately 23.7 million Americans had diabetes in 2011 (more than 10% of the adult population), and this is expected to grow to 29.6% by 2030. The cost of diabetes to the U.S. economy is enormous: the American Diabetes Association estimates that more than $174 billion per annum is spent on this disease, including $116 billion in excess medical expenditures and $58 billion in reduced national productivity. That's about 1.25% of stated GDP. People diagnosed with diabetes, on average, have medical costs that are approximately 2.3 times higher than those without the disease. Indirect costs, meanwhile, include increased absenteeism, reduced productivity, and lost productive capacity due to premature death. Why is this shameful? Because diabetes is largely a behaviorally acquired disease, not genetic, with most types avoidable with proper diet and exercise. Ironically, while many Americans spend the first 50 years of their lives over-consuming and pumping up GDP as a result, GDP will get another boost when those same Americans are forced to enter the health care system and seek treatment.

Worse still, only some of those sick Americans will get the absolute best health care in the world. Others—50 million, to be exact—have only limited access to affordable care. For a nation that ranks near the top in GDP per capita, this is an outrage. African-American males, one segment of the population with disproportionately poor access to affordable care, can expect to live 5.4 years less than white males. A similar gap exists between African-American and white women. In addition, African-Americans are less likely to have health insurance. As a result, they are likely to be treated later in the course of controllable diseases than those with better access to care.

This is not really an issue of racism so much as classism, and it leads back to the need for better GINI figures. There is, unsurprisingly, a direct correlation between U.S. poverty and life expectancy. The life expectancy of African-American men, sadly, is not only cut short by health but also by crime. According to the Bureau of Justice Statistics, despite being only some 13% of the population, African-Americans comprise 49% of all murder victims in America. Improving education, which makes people healthier, coupled with creating a small health care safety net through legislation such as the Affordable Care Act, has the potential to improve health. In turn, economic mobility and reduced crime rates could improve health and life expectancy in a virtuous circle.

Some argue that fixing the broken U.S. health care system is impossible, since the problems are so vast. Does America have the political will and technical know-how necessary to rein in skyrocketing drug prices, manage doctor liabilities, and enact meaningful tort law reform? Can it end the American Medical Association's monopoly on doctor training, lower barriers for drug approval, and get people out of emergency rooms and into better care? Unlike any other health care paradigm in the world, the American system is less about health and wellness and more about incentive groups: doctors, lawyers, large pharmaceutical companies, medical equipment manufacturers, insurance companies, hospital administrators, nurses, and last and very much least, patients.

Americans spend, on average, $6,500 per capita on health care annually, which is about twice what is spent in wealthy countries like the UK, France, Japan, Germany, Australia, and Canada. Yet this has not resulted in better life expectancy or health. Cuba, for example, has roughly the same life expectancy as America despite spending about 1/10th on health care per capita with only 1/9th as much GDP per capita. Less consumption, more frequent check-ups with doctors, and the second highest doctor-to-patient ratio in the world all add up to an interesting culture of better health in Cuba. Moreover, with a socialized national system of health care, Cuba doesn't have the life expectancy gaps discussed previously in places like metro Los Angeles.

According to several studies, America spends 95% of all health expenditure on medical treatment and only about 5% on preventative care. That's a big reason why U.S. health care costs are so high. Americans, especially poor Americans, wait until someone is sick before visiting the doctor.

The Centers for Disease Control and Prevention noted in 2011 that treatment for chronic diseases, including diabetes, obesity, and cardiovascular disease, accounted for more than 75% of U.S. expenditures on health care, or roughly $2.3 trillion. Yet much of this is linked to access: the National Prevention, Health Promotion, and Public Health Council notes that roughly 50% of Americans don't have access to preventative care. Instead of routinely going for check-ups and screenings, many Americans simply wait until they have problems, with the uninsured often going to expensive hospital emergency rooms for routine medical problems.

The sprawling system is plagued by spiraling costs that some argue waste up to one-third of all expenditures—perhaps a trillion dollars, or some 6% of GDP. Critics cite inordinate expenses in the last years of life that serve neither patients nor their families well. Others, like Sharon Brownlee in her excellent book, *Overtreated,* note that the system is inherently unreliable. While the well-insured have access to any number of procedures and are often over-treated, the uninsured and under-insured regularly go without preventative care.

The U.S. also suffers from supply/demand imbalances, as noted earlier. Far too small to meet foreseeable trends, America's current health care workforce and infrastructure are limited by an archaic guild system, the American Medical Association (AMA), which has not adequately prepared for future health care demand in America. Almost every other country in the world has systems that are public in nature. Public universities educate doctors and nurses, and the sizes of such programs are state-directed, not run by guilds like the AMA. The U.S. employs about 6.6 doctors per 100,000 in the population, while OECD countries average 10.6. A similar shortage exists in nursing: the U.S. has roughly 8.1 nurses per 1,000 patients, compared to 12-14 per 1,000 in most OECD countries.

As these and other problems related to American health take on increasing importance, the Information Age stands poised to provide innovative approaches to research, to create mass and customized solutions, and to actually change policy based upon evidence. Most health policy thinking in the U.S. has been conducted by various ideological camps, each of which defends its favored positions and attacks almost all ideas coming from others. The country desperately needs unbiased, non-partisan solutions to its current and future health policy problems.

Health care is one of the most contentious issues being debated in America. And, despite being one of the largest segments of the economy, the industry as a whole seems to operate outside the laws of supply and demand. My recommendations on how to address the problem, therefore, are simple: first, decrease the demand for health care, and second, increase its supply.

1. Preventative Health versus Remediation. The best way to curb medical expenditures is to avoid problems in the first place. Teaching children during primary school the benefits of healthy eating and moderate exercise—and the perils of smoking—has the potential to yield long-lasting benefits, not only for individuals but for the nation as a whole. The National Institutes of Health (NIH) notes that if Americans simply ate better, exercised, and didn't smoke, they could reduce their health costs by as much as one-third.

2. Digitizing and Centralizing Medical information. The U.S. spends vast amounts of money on curing cancer and late-in-life chronic illnesses. Too often, Americans neglect routine screenings and visits that could keep them healthier in the long run. An electronic medical record system could provide alerts to health professionals that patients are in need of a check-up. Basic information on a patient's medical e-file—age, family history, and gender—could be compared against a database of best practices and governmental guidelines, and the system could alert the doctor when a patient is due for a flu shot, Mammogram, or dozens of other diagnostic tests. Some systems may even be able to send patients an e-mail reminding them to schedule the appointment. And under the Affordable Care Act, such preventative care is covered under most health insurance plans and includes no out-of-pocket costs.

Big Data should also lead us to "smart cards." In Taiwan, for example, every citizen has a card encoded with his or her entire medical history. Present it to any doctor, and the doctor will know every health concern you've had since you were born. Along with improving information access, smart cards reduce administrative paperwork, since medical providers can use them to bill insurers or government directly for their services. Massachusetts is set to move towards a similar system, but such a program should be rolled out nationally which could save billions in productivity and more accurate health delivery.

3. More Medical and Nursing Schools. Milton Friedman presciently warned back in 1961 that the American Medical Association was a government-sanctioned cartel that would raise health care costs and diminish quality. He was right.

During the 1980s and 1990s, only one new medical school was established in the U.S. There are roughly 135 accredited medical schools in the country, but more are needed. As mentioned above, the U.S. is currently experiencing a shortage of doctors and nurses. In particular, America needs more general practitioner doctors, not specialists, but the number of specialists continues to grow thanks to the AMA, which has encouraged doctors to choose fields in which they can charge more for expensive procedures. In short, this has created monopolistic supply-demand imbalances – and have probably pushed up health care costs. According to a 2007 McKinsey study, U.S. doctors make twice as much as their OECD peers, which has a ripple effect throughout the American health care system, increasing expenses at every turn. In most countries around the world, medical schools are public institutions and the government determines how many doctors are needed. If the U.S government sanctioned more and sized medical schools, targeting the best mix of generalists and specialists in specific geographies based on demographic and immigration trends, it could increase the supply of available doctors, nurses, and other regulated health professionals – and hopefully bring down average costs.

Policy Area #5: Brave New Infrastructure and Energy

Along with human capital, a modern country requires physical capabilities—infrastructure and energy—for economic health. In the U.S., despite a steadily rising GDP, the country's infrastructure is literally rotting.

Hurricane Katrina in 2005 and the Northeast blackout of 2003 exposed America's aging infrastructure, which continues to penalize the U.S. economy. Crumbling and congested roads, clogged-up ports, an outmoded air traffic control system, and an unreliable electrical grid have cost the U.S. lives, not to mention billions, if not trillions, in lost income and productivity. Quality of life, too, has taken a hit, its deterioration measurable in the millions of hours lost to traffic congestion and detours.

America's Founding Fathers knew that great nations need great infrastructures. Thomas Jefferson's Secretary of Treasury Albert Gallatin, while delivering his *Report on Roads and Canals* in 1808, the first such comprehensive infrastructure study in the nation, declared that only the federal government could remove obstacles to transportation. The resulting plan led to a canal system that helped move goods in the 19th century. In 1862, Congress passed the Pacific Railroad Act to finance the transcontinental railroads. The legislation contained a variety of incentives, as well as rights to minerals, including coal for the steam engines. In the 20th century, FDR's Works

Progress Administration and Eisenhower's national highway system each expanded the infrastructure.

The U.S. needs a bold plan to compete in the 21st century. According to the World Economic Forum's Global Competitiveness Report, an important comparative study that uses 111 composite statistics, America is ranked only 25th in the world. For an even bleaker examination of America's national capabilities, take a look at the *2013 Report Card for America's Infrastructure*, the fifth in a series that began in 1988. When the first report was released, America's infrastructure earned a "C," along with various recommendations that have essentially gone ignored. Now computed by the *American Society of Civil Engineers*, the 2013 report gave the U.S. an overall "D+" as follows:

Aviation	D
Bridges	C+
Dams	D
Potable Water	D
Energy	D+
Hazardous Waste	D
Inland Waterways	D-
Levees	D-
Ports	C
Public Parks and Recreation	C-
Rail	C+
Roads	D
Schools	D
Solid Waste	B-
Transit	D
Wastewater	D

The Department of Transportation reports that freight bottlenecks cost the American economy $200 billion a year—more than 1% of formal GDP. The Federal Aviation Administration, meanwhile, estimates that air traffic delays shave approximately $33 billion off the economy every year. And every year the infrastructure is ignored, the danger grows. The grass-roots organization Transportation for America notes that some 67,000 bridges are structurally deficient. These bridges, which total more than 10% of such structures in the country, serve approximately 283 million people *each day*. According to the American Society of Civil Engineers, the U.S. will need to spend a remarkable $3.6 trillion, or roughly 25% of its annual GDP, on infrastructure by 2020 just to get the country back to average.

Anyone who owns a house knows the consequences of procrastinating when it comes to maintenance and repairs. The longer we wait to address a particular problem, the worse it gets—and the more it costs to fix. So we either pay now or pay multiples later. America can't wait any longer. Globalization doesn't sleep. Many countries are continuously upgrading their competitiveness. While America has been spending roughly 2.5% of GDP on infrastructure per annum, Europe has spent roughly 5%. Some emerging economies like Singapore and China have been spending 7% to 9% for decades.

Energize Ourselves

Stanford historian Ian Morris and others note that access to cheap and abundant energy has been essential to economic competiveness and dominance, which is one reason why China has been scouting the world for long-term energy supplies this past decade. Today more than ever, steady power is a prerequisite for the energy-intensive manufacturing and computing that underpins any advanced economy. But for the last 40 years, America has relied heavily on overseas energy imports, which has strained the country's trade deficit, led to volatile prices, shaped its foreign policy, and cost it *trillions* in the process. By living in some of the largest heated and air-conditioned houses in the world, often in suburbs that require private car transport, Americans use double the energy per capita of a typical Japanese or European person—and quadruple the global average.

But there is hope: U.S. per capita energy consumption has remained relatively stable and has even fallen since reaching an all-time high in 1979. The Energy Information Administration (EIA) notes that in 2012 America registered the lowest carbon emission levels since 1992, its output dropping nearly 15% from its peak in 2007 and 2008. And, according to a November 2012 report by the EIA, there is new hope on the supply side, as well: high oil prices and new technologies could enable the U.S. to not only become energy independent but also a potential exporter in the coming decades. A 2012 Congressional Research Service report confirmed as much, noting that U.S. natural gas reserves have climbed 72% since 2000 and 49% since 2005. Shale gas, a relatively recent development, now comprises 32% of America's gas reserves and is a growing part of gas production.

This could be an economic game changer, considering how much of America's economy and foreign policy has been entangled with foreign energy for the last 40 years. These changes on both the supply and demand side will strengthen America's global competitiveness and economic standing. Indeed, increases in domestic gas supplies, coupled with slower energy demand, have already brought down prices dramatically from $12 per million BTU in mid-2008 to approximately $3.50 in 2013. The U.S. government projects that the average price will stay below $6 for another decade, particularly as hydraulic fracking increases natural gas supplies even more. And America's cost advantage is substantial.

Cheap energy, coupled with rising labor costs in many emerging markets, could bring back some heavy manufacturing to the U.S., which in turn should help America's trade deficit, as well. In fact, a PricewaterhouseCoopers report suggests that, due to the benefits of cheaper energy and the demand for products used to extract natural gas, increased natural gas from shale could lead to about one million more U.S. manufacturing jobs by 2025. As stated earlier, the U.S. will need more cheap energy. With the advent of exascale computing, which will be used by every sector of the U.S. economy, there will be enormous electricity demand for cooling.

There are already encouraging signs that America's new energy mix is reducing carbon emissions. CO_2 levels in 2012 fell to levels not seen since 1990. How? The U.S. used to generate about half of its electricity from coal and roughly 20% from gas, which emits 45% less carbon per energy unit than coal. In recent years, those numbers have changed, first slowly and now dramatically. In 2012 coal's share in power generation fell to 32%—roughly the same as natural gas, according to the EIA.

The question is not whether but *when* America is prepared to address its infrastructure issues. With record low interest rates and excess labor from the housing construction slowdown, the time for repair and expansion is now. A brave new infrastructure plan would not only help make the U.S. more productive and efficient in the long term but would also stimulate jobs, especially in the construction sector, one of the worst hit by the recession, and would create a multiplier effect throughout the economy. Three government policies to put America on a sustainable path include:

1. New Infrastructure Stimulus. Implement the American Society of Civil Engineer's $3.6 trillion infrastructure plan over 12 years, combining public and private monies. Through a variety of incentives, approximately $1.2 trillion of federal funds could be matched with $2.4 trillion of private investment to create more than five million jobs and bring the U.S. back to pre-crisis employment levels. The Congressional Budget Office notes that infrastructure spending is a 1.6X multiplier to the economy, with some critical transportation and energy projects producing even larger multiplier effects.

2. Establish a National Infrastructure Bank. To spur expansion, government will need to mobilize private capital through the financial markets as it has in the past. Michael Lind and Sherle Schwenninger of the New America Foundation have called for a federal Works Progress Administration-style institution to help finance this build-out. With historically low interest rates, a combination of public and private investment could reap attractive economic dividends in the coming decades. Again, there is ample historical evidence of government supporting infrastructure. Strategic sectors, including the Farm Credit System, as well as Ginnie Mae and Freddie Mac, have supported the economy in the past. But now, instead of buttressing the housing construction sector, America could cultivate world-class public infrastructure.

3. Develop a Comprehensive Energy Plan. It's been 40+ years since the first energy shock in 1973, and the U.S. has ignored its supply/demand imbalance for too long. America needs a big-picture plan that includes incentives for boosting conservation *and* domestic energy production from both natural gas and renewables. Reliable domestic energy could help provide competitive advantages and reshape America's foreign policy posture in the 21st century. While gas is generally cleaner than coal, the U.S. also needs to pursue renewables such as wind, water, and solar power, along with other technologies. Addressing climate change, air pollution, water pollution, and energy insecurity requires a large-scale conversion to a mix of cleaner, more reliable lower cost energy sources. It also requires an increase in energy efficiency. In this respect, cheap natural gas should be viewed as a "bridge" fuel until renewables become cheaper. Similarly, policies geared toward greater conservation, such as continually improving Corporate Average Fuel Economy (CAFE) numbers, would help cars rely less and less on oil. A 2009 McKinsey report found America could save $1.2 trillion through 2020 by investing $520 billion in industrial, residential, and commercial improvements, such as sealing leaky building ducts and replacing inefficient household appliances with new, energy-saving models. Some of these improvements could be implemented through new regulation, as with CAFE standards for cars, along with tax incentives.

Brave new infrastructure and energy plans could help the U.S. remain globally competitive. More importantly, they have the potential to improve the quality of life in America through less pollution, lower carbon emissions, cleaner drinking water, faster commutes, fewer traffic casualties, and safer roads, bridges, and tunnels.

Policy #6: Brave New Defense

Americans automatically equate military spending with "defense." But a large part of so-called defense spending doesn't go toward enhancing military capability or making the U.S. safer. Instead, over the last 15 years, the U.S. has significantly increased spending on veterans' health care costs, administrative expenses, and overseas engagements in return for arguably limited strategic value. Such costs soar even further if we take a more inclusive view of military-related spending and include items that fall outside the formal Defense Department budget.

What the U.S. spends on traditional military readiness, meanwhile, is also worth examining. Is the American military properly configured to meet today's challenges? The world has changed drastically since World War II, and military spending priorities should reflect that. While the U.S. certainly needs to be secure, its defense spending, which currently exceeds $750 billion, needn't amount to 50% of all government discretionary spending. Some military spending has already been set by past decisions, but the portion of the budget that can still change bears further scrutiny.

As with other indicators, military costs can be described with headline numbers: approximately $553 billion in 2012 for the Defense Department. But other, related figures are often left out of the total. For example, veterans' benefits total another $90 to $100 billion per year and are recurring. As long as there are soldiers, America will incur similar costs. Indeed, the long offensives in Afghanistan and Iraq—and the relatively low fatality rates—mean that the U.S. will be paying expensive benefits for decades to come. Anyone who wants to understand the math should read Joe Stiglitz and Linda Bilmes's excellent analysis, *The Three Trillion Dollar War*.

Then there is the interest on debt incurred for previous military spending, which, though difficult to quantify, is estimated at between $60 and $100 billion annually. It's easy to forget that the deficits built during George W. Bush's presidency totaled some *$5 trillion*. The Department of Homeland Security, created after 9/11, now has a budget of $60 billion, and the State Department another $50 billion. Special allocations to the War on Terror over the last decade, though buried in the budget, add another $50 to $100 billion. During the heavy engagements in Iraq and Afghanistan, these figures sometimes topped $20 billion *per month*. Indeed, adjusted for inflation, these defense costs have actually swollen since 9/11 by some 50%.

This raises many interesting questions. Since 9/11 the U.S. has increased its military spending but hasn't adequately shifted the allocation of resources to reflect new threats. Shouldn't 9/11 have served as a wake-up call to prepare for 21st century conflicts? In the age of information-driven globalization, how much should America spend to keep its citizens safe? Will the risks and threats of the past be the same in the future? Is this $750+ billion way too much, or way too little? Is the U.S. overpaying for the security that it's getting? Does it need brave new policies in this arena?

To begin answering these questions, we need to revisit the thinking behind defense. Is it really about "defending" against foreign attack, or is defense a more complicated, multifaceted problem? A Cato Institute study observed in 2009:

> *The U.S. military is supposed to contain China; transform failed states so they resemble ours; chase terrorists; train various militaries to do so; protect sea lanes; keep oil cheap; democratize the Middle East; protect European, Asian, and Middle Eastern states from aggression and geopolitical competition; popularize the United States via humanitarian missions; respond to natural disasters at home and abroad; secure cyberspace; and more. The forces needed to accomplish this litany of aspirations can never be enough. Hence, neither can the defense budget. But the relationship between these objectives and the end they are supposed to serve—the protection of Americans and their welfare—is tenuous.*

As the Cato authors note, the list of objectives is long but not necessarily the domain of a trained military. If we consider all these goals as part of "defense," we can make the argument that you can never spend too much. But the truth is that, in the end, there is a price tag for security, and finite resources to pay for it. The more for security means mean less money for education and health, less for infrastructure, and less for diplomacy or other activities that can actually diffuse and pre-empt conflict more effectively. Moreover, military costs have a nasty habit of accumulating even after the conflict is over, when veterans' benefits need dispensing and debt payments need to be made. While there are many debatable approaches to strategic defense, there is a one-word strategy that can make a trillion-dollar difference in spending: restraint. That is, by selectively deciding *not to enter* into a military conflict hastily, we can dramatically reduce current and future defense costs.

Compared to those of the past, security risks in the modern world look and feel different. America has no lurking superpower to face. Russia and China might be seen as potential rivals, but they spend a fraction of what the U.S. does on its military. Even when interest payments and other special allocations are ignored, the U.S. still outspends China three-to-one. In the 21st century, conflicts are more likely to involve drones or surgical strikes than they are to comprise conventional battles between opposing armies, air forces, or navies. In the age of information, technology, and globalization, the U.S. needs to be smarter in defense, which requires "smart power."

Joseph Nye and Susan Nossel coined the term "smart power" almost a decade ago in two influential *Foreign Affairs* articles, but the concept behind it goes back much further. Carl von Clausewitz's seminal work *On War* described in 1832 two broad philosophies to defeat an enemy: "moral qualities and effects," which later came to be called "soft power," and "military force," or "hard power." The 21st century will demand new and more advanced combinations of both.

As part of a smart power initiative, the Center for Strategic and International Studies (CSIS) recommends reliance not only on the Defense Department but on a variety of other government, private sector, non-governmental, and multilateral organizations to detect, diffuse, and pre-empt many conflicts. As CSIS notes, "Power is the *ability to influence* others to get a desired outcome. Historically, power has been measured by such criteria as population size and territory, natural resources, economic strength, military force, and social stability." The ability to influence is the key. While the U.S. boasts the world's largest and most diversified economy *and* the largest and most expensive military (with expenditures larger than the next 13 countries combined), it's not always successful in using its power to influence the rest of the world.

Why is such a brave new philosophy like smart power important? First, it attempts to redefine "defense." In the past, America often operated from a simple adage: "the best defense is a good offense." Today, military firepower would form just one pillar of a redefined defense, not the sole foundation. New philosophies will be needed to pave the way for a myriad of military savings. The following four innovations, already explored by CSIS and other Washington think tanks, have the potential to redefine American defense for the 21st century:

1. Information Technology and Innovation. Military intelligence is based on solid information, but throughout much of military history, decisions have been based on poor data. Many offensives, including America's recent push into Iraq, were based on sketchy information. Going forward, if the U.S. hopes to replace brute force with more efficient and less costly approaches, it must adopt a "big data" approach to its military capabilities. Exascale computing, as an integral part of the defense puzzle, can help military experts look at and analyze a variety of data sources, as well as run simulations and cost/benefit analyses to help shape policy. Other emerging technologies in robotics, biotechnology, and artificial intelligence can also play an important role in remaking the military, which, in turn, will have to make advances in combatting those very same technologies, should they fall into the wrong hands, whether terrorist or criminal.

Contrary to conventional wisdom, brave new 21st century security may be cheaper than in the past. For example, counterterrorism costs much less than multi-billion dollars of tanks, submarines, fighter planes, ground troops and nuclear weapon systems. Modern terrorists don't fight conventionally like countries. They are lightly armed and fight clandestinely. In the future they may fight remotely from thousands of miles away. The difficulty is not killing or capturing these 21st century enemy combatants but rather finding them and diffusing attacks before they are launched. According to most experts, the best approach in counterterrorism includes robust intelligence and policing.

Interestingly, such an approach plays into America's strength as a high-tech innovator of information and technology. The most useful

21st century military tools, moreover, are relatively cheap. Couple surveillance technologies[7] and drones with elite special forces, such as those used to hunt and kill Osama Bin Laden, and suddenly the U.S. can maintain a cheaper but far more effective defense posture. Indeed, the future of cross-border warfare and threats lies in the tech space, particularly global networks, advanced robotics, artificial intelligence, and biotech. Already we've seen glimpses of this—unmanned planes gathering information and images, satellites intercepting communications, naval ships launching missiles from hundreds of miles away. Remote pilots sitting halfway around the world can kill enemy combatants with the click of a mouse, but this is just a sneak peek at what's coming. As nanotechnology develops, science fiction will become science fact: insect sized drones capable of surveillance and intelligence gathering for weapon strikes; molecularly manufactured microbes and viruses that can devastate populations while being controlled from different continents; and info-tech hacking programs that can disrupt power grids, banking systems, and anything else that is networked in the Information Age.

America has long been in the vanguard of technology, and its military has always had close ties to the private sector and universities, propelling research and development. As mentioned above, maintaining such a position in the world will require strengthening STEM studies in our schools. The military, meanwhile, must reorient its priorities so that, when it comes to formulating a smart defense budget, advanced research and technology are seen as more important than a fleet of expensive fighter jets or submarines.

2. Economic and Human Capacity Development. We forget that there are still more than a billion people who live in poverty in developing countries. Such poverty can isolate people, turning them into hotbeds for terrorism and instability. Trading nations integrated through supply chains rarely engage in war. Boosting trade boosts wealth globally and, like development, reduces the chances for

---

[7] Interestingly, the 2013 National Security Administration scandal involving Edward Snowden highlighted how the United States has already been implementing surveillance not only against known enemies – but also allies.

military conflict. Most conflict in the world tends to occur in countries where GDP is roughly 1/20th of U.S. GDP. These countries, rather than continuing on indefinitely with the spaghetti bowl of bilateral agreements that have evolved over the past decade, would greatly benefit from re-launching the Doha round of multilateral trade talks. Increasing the benefits of trade for all people globally—and getting them invested in the global trading system—is essential to reducing military risks. Trade, as we've discussed, is also highly linked to human capital. Therefore, fostering more support for educational and health efforts through multilateral institutions like the World Bank, Asian Development Bank, and African Development Bank could pre-empt future military threats while advancing human capabilities in developing countries.

3. Alliances, Partnerships, and Institutions. To address challenges facing the globalizing world, America will need to maintain a collective security stance, because the problems of the 21st century are too large and complex for the U.S. to go it alone. That means working with multilateral organizations like the United Nations, despite the fact that none are perfect and most need a dramatic overhaul. Groups like the U.N. can help ensure safety and save the U.S. billions in military spending through greater shared peacekeeping and peace-building efforts, along with the development of a counterterrorism capability. Note that the U.N. is a cheap line item in America's defense expenses—less than $3.5 billion for 2012—one that could be leveraged through cooperation with many other countries. Other alliances, such as NATO, could be formed in Asia and viewed as "force multipliers" to complement U.S. military power.

Moreover, the April 2013 U.N. treaty aimed at regulating the enormous global trade in conventional weapons could also serve as a catalyst for further regulating the broader global arms trade. Another way to curb global military spending is to limit access to weapons. In the big picture, the $60 billion in cross-border arms trade is an extremely small percentage of the world economy. Surely the economic, physical, and psychic costs of arming future terrorists and U.S. enemies warrant more arms bans. The U.S. should not be pennywise and pound foolish. An economy of $16+ trillion can do without the miniscule profits gleaned from industries that could cost hundreds of times in military expenses down the line.

4. Public Diplomacy. Part of smart power's "soft" side is improving global access to international knowledge, learning, and culture around the world. It means cultivating a more optimistic and cooperative mindset, particularly in emerging markets. By upping the State Department's budget, which is currently about 1/16th that of the Defense Department's, and expanding educational exchanges and diplomatic organizations like the Peace Corps, the U.S. can help push forward best practices and institutions to accelerate greater civil society throughout the world.

In short, brave new "smart power" would reduce "hard" military expenditures while increasing "soft" approaches, such as counterterrorism, diplomacy, global development, and accelerated trade integration. Moreover, greater reliance on technology could help the U.S. pre-empt and/or diffuse crises before they escalate into true military conflict. Greater reliance on multilateral alliances and institutions and greater respect for international laws, meanwhile, coupled with strategic restraint, could help the U.S. avoid costly military bills. Taken together with earlier recommendations for improved information, infrastructure, and domestic energy production, "smart power" can help America regain broader global influence at a price the U.S. can afford.

Policy Area #7: Brave New Taxation

Perhaps no issue is more controversial than taxation in America, and rightly so. America was founded on the belief that there can be "no taxation without representation." But what should taxes fund? Sure, the U.S. will always need taxes to "provide for the common defense," but increasingly part of America's common defense is economic competitiveness. Without ensuring that the U.S. economy is globally capable, America will actually be "weak" in the modern sense of security.

Unfortunately, the U.S. tax structure is a hodgepodge of ad hoc policies at the federal, state, and local levels that has become an enormous headache and time-sink for American taxpayers. It would be naïve to think that tax reform can be easy, but if the U.S. can shed conventional wisdom and use a *Moneyball* data approach, its citizens can begin a dialogue about using taxation as an important catalyst for brave new policies for 21st century America.

The Cornerstone of Reform: Progressive Taxation

A cornerstone for brave new America, tax reform would provide an opportunity to help reshape government and policies, strip away legacy problems and inconsistencies, and still provide for equal opportunities, better health, more resilient jobs, and more secure retirements. This won't be easy. But if Americans don't first admit they have significant tax problems, they cannot begin to fix them. And there is a lot to fix.

In constructing brave new taxation, we should strive for a fair system, one that asks Americans to contribute based on their ability to pay. This is called "progressive" taxation, and it's a theory rooted in the biblical notion that a few pennies from a poor woman costs her more than many pieces of gold from a rich man. In theory, America's tax code is progressive, but in practice it is not. As billionaire Warren Buffet reminded Americans during the 2012 presidential elections, his secretary pays almost double the federal tax rate that he does.

Interestingly Adam Smith, the father of modern capitalism, is also the father of progressive taxation. As he wrote in *The Wealth of Nations*, "It is not very unreasonable that the rich should contribute to the public expense, not only in proportion to their revenue, but something more than in that proportion."

The American founders also believed in progressive taxation, asserting that over time it would help lessen the inequality that they had witnessed in Europe. In a 1785 letter to James Madison, Thomas Jefferson wrote of "silently lessening the inequality of property" by exempting "all from taxation below a certain point, and to tax the higher portions of property in geometrical progression as they rise." In

1790, he noted that the collection of taxes might someday fall 100% on wealthy Americans, reiterating it again in a 1811 letter: "The farmer will see his government supported, his children educated, and the face of this country made a paradise by the contributions of the rich alone, *without his being called on to spend a cent from his earnings.*"

In this respect, progressive taxation corresponds with America's sense of fairness, because a dollar in taxes costs a poor person much more than a dollar from a rich person. For a poor American, paying more taxes means foregoing food, heating, a car repair, or other basic necessities. But for the wealthy, paying more in taxes doesn't really diminish their comfort. They have the ability to pay more.

A regressive system, on the other hand, raises taxes from people who have the fewest resources, which has been a growing problem in recent years. As we've discussed, the wealthiest 1% of Americans have more income than the poorest 40% combined. And the top 20% of Americans earn almost as much as the remaining 80% combined. This has created an unstable economy and an unbalanced tax base.

The richest 1% of American households saw their average pre-tax income rise by 281% in the 21 years from 1979 to 2007 (adjusted for inflation). Meanwhile, middle-income earnings grew by 25% over the same period, and the poorest 20% saw their real pretax incomes grow by just 16%. Small reductions in capital gains and estate taxes, coupled with booming asset prices, helped exacerbate the trend and create the inequality and growing GINI.

Many conservatives cite the infamous Laffer Curve and note that, if we tax people at too high a rate, people will work less, tax collection won't be greater, and GDP will suffer. This has never been proven, and indeed, the climate today is far more favorable to the rich than it was in the early 20th century. In fact, tax rates once topped more than 90% of income for top earners. Today they're approximately 40%. The Clinton Administration actually raised taxes, which led to a period of GDP growth and job creation. Others claim that higher taxation stifles entrepreneurial activity. Nonsense. It's highly doubtful that Mark Zuckerberg, Steve Jobs, or Bill Gates would have been any less innovative if income tax were a few percentage points higher. And as

Warren Buffett reminded us by noting his secretary paid a higher percentage in tax than he did, the problem is not that U.S. tax rates are too high; it's that that most rich Americans don't pay anywhere close to the country's top rate of approximately 40%. There are too many breaks and incentives that make the American system inherently regressive.

The Great Tax Divide

When it comes to taxation, an enormous philosophical divide exists in America. Libertarians and conservatives want to limit government and keep taxes low, while progressives prefer more tax and redistribution. But America now functions in a globalized world. As a country, the U.S. is only as strong as its weakest links, and as we've seen, America's weakest links now—infrastructure and human capital—are in need of serious repair. When rethinking tax policies and how America might improve its competiveness, a competitive analysis, similar to the kind made by a corporation, is warranted. If we look at the OECD since 1979, tax rates in the U.S. have generally been lower than in most developed countries. In the last decade, America's position has continued to fall. In 2010, the U.S. was ranked 32nd out of 34 countries in the OECD, with only Mexico and Chile claiming lower tax receipts as a percentage of GDP. While libertarians would laud this trend, it actually explains the growing inequality and federal deficit woes that continue to make headlines in America. The U.S. has not taxing enough relative to its past, current and future needs.

For the first time since World War II, federal tax revenue in the U.S. accounted for less than 15% of GDP for 2010, 2011, and 2012. And while tax rates have fallen to levels not seen since 1950, GDP, corporate profits, and stocks markets are at all-time highs. In 2012, the S&P 500 averaged $109 in earnings per share, beating 2007's previous record of $103 and doubling the $55 at the height of the U.S. tech bubble. How is it that companies can post record profits while government is running nearly a $1 trillion operating deficit?

Corporate taxes have declined from 7.2% of GDP in 1945 to less than 2%. Taxes on the wealthiest segment of the economy have also plummeted, thanks to a combination of lower income tax rates, lower capital gains rates, and lower estate taxes. According to a General Accountability Office study, over the last 25 years, Congress has written a variety of subsidies, loopholes, and other alterations into the corporate and individual tax codes with a total value now exceeding $1 trillion per annum, or more than 6% of GDP.

The problems described earlier—America's declining mojo, rising GDP, growing social anxiety, and increasing inequality—can be seen in the changing complexion of federal taxation. As the chart below illustrates, there has been a gradual shift away from corporate, excise, and estate taxes toward payroll taxes, which has placed a heavier burden on the shoulders of ordinary Americans.

Figure 16.

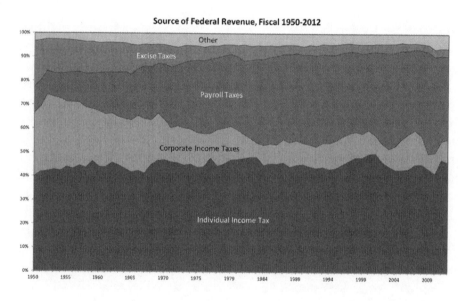

Now at first glance this might not seem like a big problem, but payroll taxes are inherently *regressive*: those with low and middle incomes pay more in payroll tax than those with high incomes, on average. The cap on wages subject to the Social Security tax means that affluent Americans pay a smaller percentage of their incomes on this tax. Those same Americans tend to earn a greater share of their incomes from capital gains, dividends, and other investments that are not subject to payroll taxes. So yes, the top 20% of Americans pay the most in federal "income" tax, but payroll taxes weigh more heavily on those in the bottom 80%. Addressing this fairness question should be a priority in any tax debate.

In addition to issues of fairness, there is the sheer complexity of the U.S. tax system. Below are a few suggestions on how we can streamline the system while also improving America's capabilities over time:

1. Simplify Taxes. Shockingly, Americans spend more than nine billion hours each year doing their taxes. At roughly $20 an hour, we're talking about $180 billion in lost human productivity. In the Information Age, this should be a no-brainer to fix.

University of Chicago professor Austan Goolsbee, the former chairman of President Obama's Council of Economic Advisers, has proposed the "Simple Return" to dramatically reduce the time and money required to file taxes. Approximately two-thirds of Americans file taxes without lengthy itemization. Their income is based largely on wages from one employer and interest from one bank. For most of these filers, the IRS already receives information about their income directly from employers and banks. Gathering documents and filling out required IRS forms, along with spending money on professional tax preparation, is redundant and expensive. In essence, millions of Americans are simply copying into their tax returns information that the IRS has already received. Why not skip this unnecessary step? Goolsbee believes his Simple Return could be used by 40% of Americans, for whom it could save up to 225 million hours each year. Several states, including California, Maine, and Massachusetts, are already using versions of the system.

2. Raise Standard Deduction, Limit Total Deductions. Another simple way to lessen tax burdens in the U.S. would be to lift standard personal deductions and limit total deductions for taxes, a two-pronged approach that was discussed during the 2012 presidential elections.

Lifting the current personal exemption would help those with the least incomes the most. And by capping overall deductions for wealthy Americans and raising standard exemptions to a dollar amount, the U.S. could collect more from wealthier Americans without actually raising tax rates. This is a far more democratic, progressive structure than what has evolved over the last generation.

3. Reduce Sales Taxes, Increase Taxes on Services and Luxury Goods. General sales taxes account for nearly 50% of revenues for state governments. While sales taxes seem attractive because of their potential to curb consumption, they are inherently regressive, requiring low-income taxpayers to pay more of their income in sales tax than wealthier taxpayers pay. Although many states have reduced or exempted sales tax on items like food and clothing, these taxes still hurt lower income groups the most.

Moreover, sales taxes typically apply to *goods*, such as books and radios, but not services, such as manicures and car repairs. When most state sales taxes were enacted in the 1930s, services were a relatively small part of American consumer spending. But in the 21st century, services now represent about two-thirds of individual consumption nationally. Expanding the tax base to include personal services would result in a slightly less regressive system, because wealthier people consume more services. Another option would be to reduce sales taxes on some items altogether, while raising taxes on certain luxury items over a certain price threshold. Cars, jewelry, watches, designer clothing—all are positional goods that are less price-sensitive. Their buyers won't be dissuaded by a couple extra percentage points of tax.

4. Revamp Corporate Tax. Through the 1950s, companies were taxed at a much higher rate than they are today—more than 50%, according to the nonpartisan Tax Policy Center. Back then, approximately one-third of federal government revenues came from corporate taxes. Today, corporate taxes are less than 40%, if companies even pay that rate.

Globalization is partially to blame for this low tax collection. In the closed world of the 1950s and 1960s, Fortune 500 companies employed hundreds of thousands of Americans, selling goods and services mostly in the U.S., and they paid billions of dollars in taxes every year. Now, with global supply chains and global consumers, companies have more latitude regarding taxable income in the U.S.

More importantly, a large loophole allows U.S. multinational operators to avoid taxes on overseas profits until the money is repatriated. This has created an incentive to keep the money offshore and help finance further global operations, which in turn costs the U.S. not only needed tax funds but also domestic jobs. According to a 2010 McKinsey report, U.S. multinationals represented less than 1% of total American companies in 2007 but accounted for roughly 19% of private sector jobs, 25% of private sector wages, 25% of private sector gross profits, 48% of total U.S. goods exported, and 74% of research and development spending. Often the money just sits idle. According to the Federal Reserve Bank of St. Louis, American corporations are now sitting on more than $1.75 trillion in excess cash overseas, much of it waiting for some kind of tax amnesty. Two organizations—the Institute for Taxation and Economic Policy and Citizens for Tax Justice—have conducted numerous studies showing that large multinationals, particularly in the technology sectors, have been able to use tax loopholes to push down their effective tax rates well below the current "sticker" price. In a highly publicized U.S. Senate investigation in May 2013, Apple Inc. was found to have paid no corporate income tax to any national government on tens of billions of dollars in overseas income from 2008 to 2012. Although perfectly legal, such a built-in subsidy has inadvertently led to more investment and job creation overseas over the last two decades. This is clearly a tax distortion that needs to be eliminated so companies will pay their fair share.

If the U.S. increases corporate tax collection to its effective rate, it should also consider eliminating double taxation of dividends. Currently, interest paid on bonds and loans can be deducted as a business expense, while dividends paid on equity cannot. In a brave new American tax system, interest income from debt, such as bonds or bank accounts, and dividends from stocks would be treated exactly the same. This could be easily accomplished by making cash dividends paid as a tax deduction for corporations, which would likely reduce the overall amount of debt companies issue—and perhaps render their capital structure more secure.

5. Social Security Reform. Social Security was another program born in Simon Kuznets's era—in 1935 to be precise—when Americans were concerned about growing poverty among the elderly during the Depression. At the time, most in the U.S. had no assets, and few private retirement programs existed. There were approximately seven working people for every one retiree, and the available data suggested Americans would retire in their early sixties and enjoy perhaps five to seven years of benefits before passing away.

Demographics have shifted dramatically since then. Americans are now, on average, seven years older than in 1950. One of the biggest informational failures of the last fifty years has been poorly predicting and understanding employment-to-population and dependency ratio trends, as discussed earlier. Indeed, while we have fixated on U3 unemployment figures, labor participation rates have declined and dependency rates have rose. America now has only three workers per retiree, and that ratio is continuing to shrink because of lower birth rates, higher life spans, and a relatively weak labor market. With Americans living approximately 80 years today, Social Security could foreseeably be paying benefits for 15 or more years, more than twice as long as originally intended. Despite rising life expectancy, however, America began paying out Social Security benefits earlier, at age 62 instead of 65, a generation ago, when it probably should have gone the other way and lifted the age by three years. Indeed, since then, the age has been raised for new workers to 67. But the U.S. still must accommodate many Baby Boomers already in the position to retire early.

Two simple solutions are available: (1) start the system later, and (2) use means-testing to limit the system to only those who truly need it. Social Security should be viewed as a generic retirement tax to help America's elderly poor. Wealthier Americans with substantial private savings and income should not be eligible for Social Security.

6. Phase-out of Mortgage Interest Deductions (MID) and Housing Related Tax Subsidies. At a time when the U.S. housing market has been so battered, it may seem sacrilegious to think about repealing the favorable tax treatment for homeownership. But it's time the U.S. stopped favoring homeowners over renters—and time to disentangle housing and education opportunities in America.

Note that Mortgage Interest Deductions (MID) was an accidental byproduct of the income tax legislation, enacted by Congress in 1913, which made all forms of interest payments tax deductible in order to help small businesses. At that time, most homes were purchased with cash, so home mortgage interest was nonexistent. Moreover, more than 99% of Americans did not earn enough income to pay taxes back then, so the deduction didn't have a big impact on tax collection. However, after the Federal Housing Administration and Fannie Mae were created in the 1930s, home mortgages became more prevalent, and mortgage interest deduction became firmly entrenched in the culture of America's nesting nation.

America's policy is a global anachronism. According to the Bank of International Settlements, the U.S. is unique among OECD countries in that it both allows mortgage interest deduction and does not tax "imputed rent," the value that homeowners receive from owning their homes instead of paying rent to a landlord. Think of it this way: owners of their houses get a deduction, but renters do not. And while approximately two-thirds of Americans own homes, one-third rent.

Despite offering the most favorable tax subsidy, the U.S. surprisingly does not enjoy a higher rate of homeownership than Canada, Australia, or United Kingdom three countries that don't tax imputed rent or allow MID. This is because the subsidy doesn't reach more than 70% of Americans who don't earn enough to use it. Instead, it accrues overwhelmingly to the wealthiest Americans, who need it the least. While the average deduction for American homeowners is actually a modest $2,000, the return for families earning more than $250,000 a year is more than 10 times higher than the return for those earning between $40,000 and $70,000. It is de facto enjoyed by the country's top 10% in incomes.

Another unintended consequence of the MID is that it drives up housing prices. Research suggests that the mortgage interest deduction inflates prices at the upper end by 10 to 15%. Therefore, the tax benefits enjoyed by homebuyers are largely offset by the higher prices they have to pay for housing. Higher prices lead to higher property taxes, which in turn lead to higher property tax deductions, which, as discussed earlier, disproportionally help the wealthy. The Office of Management and Budget noted these subsidies totaled approximately $185 billion in lost tax collection by the federal government, $30 billion of which was from property taxes in 2009 (a low tax year due to the recession). Eliminating this over time, along with implementing a long-term phase out of MID (say over 30 years), has the potential to raise more taxes, reduce housing's impact on the American economy, and even improve labor mobility over time by freeing people's livelihoods from home ownership.

7. Phase Out Property Taxes, Increase State and Local Income Taxes for Education. Likely one of the more provocative ideas in this book, a phasing out of property taxes in the U.S. is worthy of serious consideration. To improve America's overall level of public education, we'll need to somehow wean the system away from localized property tax funding, which plays an integral role in America's gap-ridden HDI numbers, growing inequality, and overdeveloped housing market, the latter of which has become too big a part of the economy. By implementing state and municipal taxes in lieu of property and sales taxes, America can build a more progressive, fairer system that, much like federal taxation, can lower taxes for poorer families and raise taxes for wealthier families. Moreover, by relying on state and local income taxes for education, the U.S. can avoid the disparities in education that are exacerbated by a property tax-based system that favors richer neighborhoods over poorer ones. If wealthier Americans don't like the public system where they live, they can always opt for private alternatives.

8. Tax Capital Gains as Ordinary Income. Supporters of lower taxes on capital gains from investments argue that a tax on capital hurts America by reducing the incentive to save and invest. They say the same thing about the tax on dividend interest income, as well. Unfortunately, this is true of all taxation. After all, taxing labor reduces everybody's incentive to wake up and go to work every morning. So why favor capital over labor? Income is income, right?

According to a 2011 Congressional Research Service study, lowering federal tax rates on capital gains income likely played a significant role in rising income inequality in America. Capital gains and other investment income were treated like wage income until 1986, when, for the next decade, the capital gains rate was reduced. In the first half of the 21st century, the rate's further reduction as part of George W. Bush's tax cuts once again coincided with rising inequality in America. The study noted that while income rose 25% from 1996 to 2006 for all Americans, it grew 74% for the top 1% and 96% for the top 0.1%. That study also found that tax cuts on capital gains were the biggest driver of the disparity. While the capital gains rate was increased from 15 to 20% at the beginning of 2013, it might take decades to reverse the inequality.

Although some say capital gains provide an incentive to invest for the long run, long-term investment in public stocks or private companies already enjoys the advantage of compounded growth; you only pay tax when you sell. The longer you don't sell, the more time an investment has to grow in value. By eliminating the subsidy on capital gains, we may actually provide an incentive for companies, public and private, to reinvest more in their businesses, qualify for immediate tax deductions, and pay less in dividends, all of which would help American long-term competitiveness and lead to more sustainable job creation.

Like tuning a piano, reforming a tax system is an ongoing process that must be revisited at regular intervals. Americans won't be able to simply reform tax law once and then forget it. The chief goal of any change, meanwhile, must be to produce more competitive people and companies, thereby ensuring a more participatory and more prosperous future.

Epilogue

On March 5, 2013, the Dow Jones stock market index hit a milestone when it passed its pre-crisis record level on October 9, 2007 of 14,164.53, recovering from a post-crisis low on March 9, 2009 of 6,547.05. By the end of 2013, the Dow had soared past 16,000, leading no small number of investors to conclude that America's post-crisis economic woes were over. Or were they?

Long considered a bellwether for the American economy, the Dow Jones – or the broader S&P, NASDAQ, or Russell indices – no longer conveys everything we need to know about the U.S. economy. Most Americans think that whatever is happening in the economy should spill over into stock markets. But conventional thinking has its limits in the 21st century.

Most Wall Street pros know stock markets reflect views on companies, not economies. As noted earlier, until the late 20th century, American companies made things in America and generally sold them in America. If companies recorded higher sales, it was largely because they sold more in America, and those sales helped pay wages that were then re-circulated into the economy. The result, at least in GDP terms: the economy grew.

But in a globalizing world of cross-border supply chains and instantaneously connected financial systems, stock markets no longer represent the Main Street economy. If companies today can boost profits by better managing their businesses—perhaps by reducing debt expense, lowering labor costs, or sourcing cheaper parts overseas—then stock prices can still rise while the American economy sputters. And what happens if companies *do* generate higher sales but those sales are overseas? Or what if the companies now operate factories overseas? Yes, these companies may be generating record earnings for shareholders, but very little of this success may accrue to the broad American economy or its workers. Many of the biggest companies in America today pay only minimal taxes in the U.S.

According to the BEA, only 55% of the S&P 500 companies' revenues and profits actually come from the United States. The rest are from abroad. Contrast that to 1950, when only 5% came from foreign sources. By 1985 the amount was still less than 15%, but globalization has now tripled that number in a brief period.

While American companies still remain some of the world's most dynamic and valuable, they do not employ Americans in the same way they did a generation ago. For decades, an old adage in variations repeated often in the mid-20th century, held true in a positive light: "As General Motors goes, so goes America." But particularly as G.M. has gone through a public bankruptcy in which the U.S. government became its largest shareholder, is the saying still applicable? Maybe so, but not necessarily in a good way.

In the 1950s and 60s, GM employed more than 650,000 workers, virtually all of whom were Americans. The company was the beacon of American manufacturing. Today GM's workforce has fallen to approximately 212,000, only 77,000 of which are Americans. The rest, including more than 50,000 in China, now GM's largest sales market, are employed overseas. Chrysler, another bankruptcy victim, also rescued by the U.S. government, only employs 40,000 in the U.S., and Ford some 65,000. That means the Big Three have seen their U.S. automotive workforce shrink from a peak of roughly 1.5 million Americans to less than 185,000. And while several foreign manufacturers like Toyota and BMW now produce in the United States, these combined workforces only total approximately 100,000. The number of people employed by the car industry in America is a fraction of what it was in the 1950s and 1960s, even though the U.S. population is now 130 million greater than in 1960.

Ironically, although the number of Americans employed by the auto industry has shrunk, the U.S. is producing more cars. America built roughly 8 million cars in 1960, but by 2012 production had risen to 10.3 million, after peaking at 12.8 million in 2000. Technology and globalization have helped car manufacturers produce more cars with less American labor. Don't believe it? Even Tesla Motors, the electric car upstart started in Silicon Valley, only employs 3,000 American workers as of late 2013. Robots, better engineering, and foreign competition (about 50% of all cars sold in America are now imported) have transformed and downsized U.S. automotive labor.

This math applies to most of new corporate America, including its three most valuable companies: Google, Apple, and Microsoft. Together they are worth $1 trillion, or about eight to 10 times the worth of GM, Ford, and Chrysler combined. Google has only 30,000 employees worldwide, yet the company is now worth some $335 billion. Apple, with 80,000 employees, is worth more than $400 billion, and Microsoft is worth a little less than $300 billion and has 99,000 employees. Many of these tech jobs, too, are overseas. In the age of information and globalization, robust American companies aren't necessarily large American employers.

While American corporate earnings may gain strength, the U.S. economy may remain structurally weak and unbalanced. In other words, the stock market no longer reflects the economy. Some argue today that a strong stock market can spur economic confidence, producing what is known as a "wealth effect." True, there's evidence that many people spend more when they see their stock accounts grow. But even with stock markets continuing to hit record highs, the U.S. economy is still struggling.

While the U.S. job market is still far from a full recovery, at least stock prices give Americans reason to cheer. Or do they? American stock ownership is neither broad nor deep. In his recent study at NYU, Professor Ed Wolff noted that some 47% of all Americans own some stock. But if we look past this headline number, we see huge concentration of ownership in America. Approximately 53% of Americans don't own any stock at all. Among those that do, only one-third held portfolios worth more than $5,000, as of 2010. It should not surprise us that the richest 5% of U.S. households own about two-thirds of all American stocks. More than 75% is owned by households that earn more than $100,000 a year. The bottom 60% own only 2.5% of outstanding shares of stock.

Meanwhile, roughly one-third of all Americans have no savings at all (and some have a negative net worth). True, two-thirds of American families own houses, and that number has risen a few percentage points since 1960. But actual net equity in homeownership—the amount of savings after mortgage debt is subtracted from market value—has been falling. Several Federal

Reserve studies since the Great Recession shows that weak markets, coupled with low down-payment mortgages and home-equity loan extraction, have left Americans with less value than they had a generation ago. Moreover, the skew of ownership shows some disparity among race, which is highly correlated with income.

It would be foolish to say that the American economy has no impact on the American stock market, and vice versa. They are clearly intertwined. But we need to remember that stock market headlines in the Wall Street Journal or on the nightly news don't necessarily move in lockstep with the economy.

Why did American stocks soar to record highs after bottoming out in early 2009? Because the U.S. economy was operating at record-breaking speed? Sadly, no. The country's GDP growth, for whatever that statistic is worth, is historically sluggish. Interestingly, this phenomenon has gone global: Europe and Japan have seen recent strong rises in their stocks markets, but their economies are possibly in worse shape than America's.

In short, an up market doesn't mean an up economy, and a down economy doesn't equal a down market. This has been true for some time, and globalization has only accentuated this fact. Many traditional policies, therefore, that are geared toward boosting corporate investment and profits, such as lowering interest rates, don't necessarily ripple through the American economy.

Few could deny that the global landscape has changed dramatically in recent years. The process of globalization has intensified exponentially, with new technologies being developed and more information becoming available each year, and we can't wish the process away. Indeed, resisting globalization is akin to resisting the laws of gravity.

We can only hope that the Information Age helps to harness globalization's potential instead of obscuring it. Economists increasingly need to devise new ways to examine and shape national economies. In fact, as discussed earlier, the whole notion of a national economy has become an anachronism. Most Americans function within largely local or regionalized economies, with a few high-flying metropolitan areas like New York, San Francisco, and Los Angeles possessing more global connections. Indeed, the globalizing world has fractionalized America, producing growing pockets of division that have led to political gridlock, unfortunately at a time when a new public policy consensus is needed. Our American democracy hangs in the balance. In a country with shameful gaps between the haves and have-nots, public policy, as always, offers a way out.

Popular economic indicators—GDP, inflation, employment, productivity—must be reexamined before we can make sense of this globalizing world. The sooner we can expand national information infrastructures, upon which our future depends, the better. In the meantime, improving our human capacities, from health care to education, should be the focus of public policies, regardless of what metric we use to measure our progress.

Will Americans wake one day to watch CNBC reporting on improved global rankings in pre-school attendance or high school completion rates? In median health statistics and broader levels of happiness? In declining GINI coefficients and higher median incomes? In the meaningful creation of secure jobs? In the highest ranked infrastructure? Or will they still fixate on stock market levels, blunt GDP expansion, and flawed employment and productivity statistics, with no concern for quality of life? Americans live in a world of 21st century technological miracles. At the same time, climate change, terrorist hotbeds, and an increase in human inequality threaten to destabilize the planet. For economics – our modern religion for organizing society – to help shepherd solutions, we will need brave new math.

Index

A

B

C

D

E

H

I

M

N

O

P

R

S

W

Z

Made in the USA
Middletown, DE
11 December 2017